MW01529013

FANTAIL FIGHTERS

By

Jerry Scutts

PHALANX
Publishing Co., Ltd.
1051 Marie Avenue
St. Paul, MN 55118 U.S.A.
612/454-0607

Copyright © 1995 by Phalanx Publishing Co., Ltd.

All rights reserved. No part of this work covered by copyright hereon may be reproduced or used in any form or by any means - graphic, electronic, or mechanical, including photocopying, recording, taping or information storage and retrieval systems - without the written permission of the publisher.

ISBN: 1-883809-00-2

Text by: Jerry Scutts

Cover design and aircraft profiles by: John Valo

Cover action art by: Marc Stewart

Published by:

Phalanx Publishing Co., Ltd.
1051 Marie Avenue West
St. Paul, MN 55118-4131 USA

Front Cover: A Solomons Island based Kingfisher locates a downed Navy Avenger in this original action art by Marc Stewart, aviation artist of Sargent, Georgia.

Rear Cover: A pair of Curtiss SO3Cs on the fantail catapults of the Cleveland Class light cruiser, *Denver,* one of a number of ships that tested the aircraft's suitability for fleet operations. (USN)

Printed in The United States of America

INTRODUCTION

During World War II, the US Navy, Marines and Coast Guard operated two main types of floatplane, the Curtiss SOC Seagull and Vought OS2U Kingfisher plus one amphibian, the Grumman J2F Duck. During the latter half of the war, the single-seat Curtiss SC-1 Seahawk entered service, to become the last aircraft ordered for duty aboard non-carrier classes of ship. In addition, the Navy and Coast Guard operated the ill-fated Curtiss SO3C Seagull which served very briefly aboard cruisers before its relegation to land bases.[1]

In terms of wartime service, the Grumman J2F Duck was the oldest, having flown for the first time on 4 May 1933. The J2F was the only US single-engined amphibian to put in front-line sea duty during hostilities, being designed primarily to provide the Navy with a "utility" service aboard aircraft carriers. Its dual wheel/float landing gear also enabled it to perform a useful rescue function in combat areas.

On 5 March 1934[2] the portly Curtiss XSOC Seagull biplane made its debut, some three months before early production J2F-1 Ducks joined VS-3 aboard the carrier *Lexington*. Despite its somewhat anachronistic appearance the SOC was one of the most reliable and well-liked floatplanes the Navy ever ordered, so much so that it was taken out of honorary retirement in 1944 to replace its would-be successor aboard some ships of the fleet.

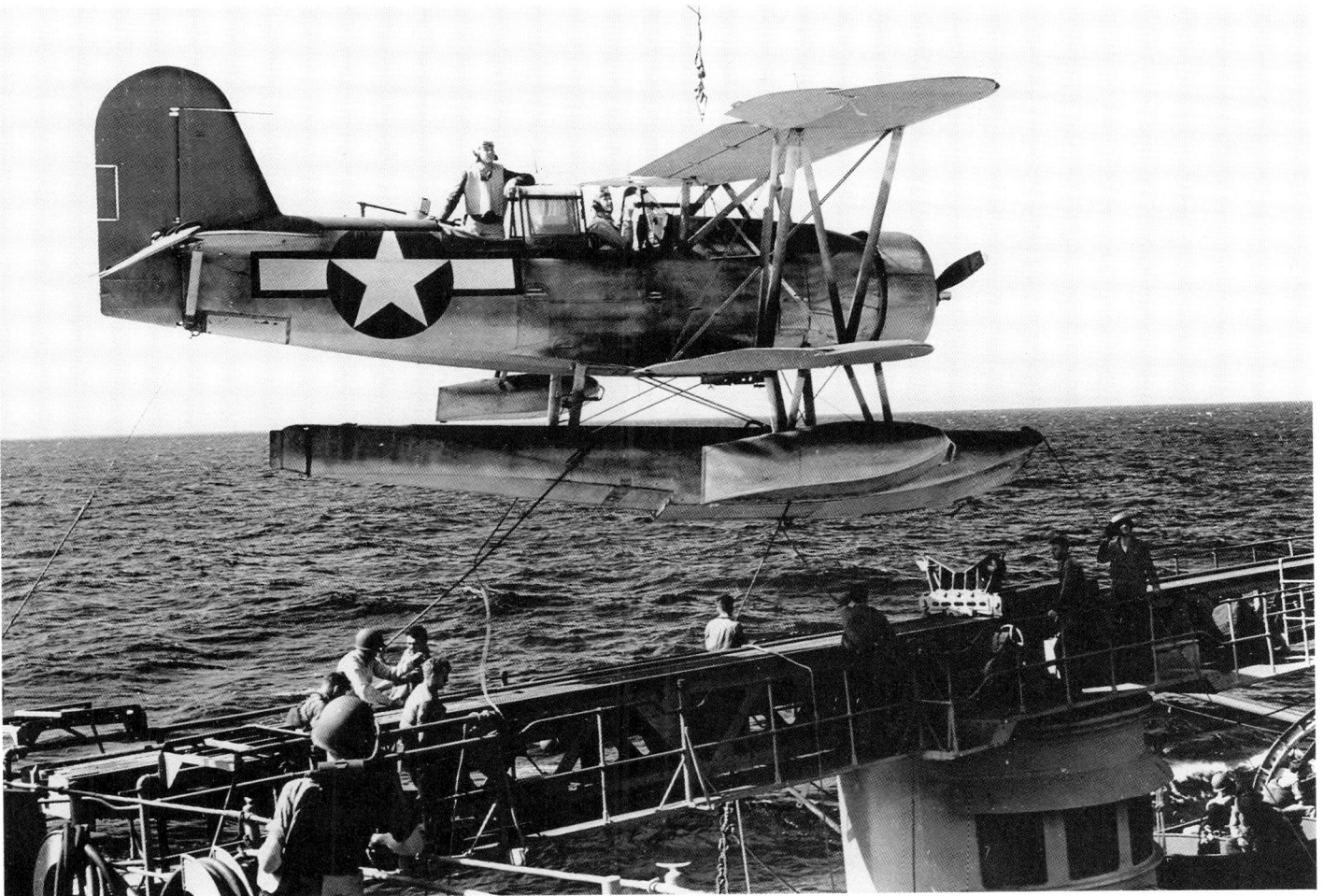

True "workhorse of the fleet" was the Curtiss SOC, seen in this view being hoisted aboard the USS *Minneapolis* (CA-36) after directing gunfire for a Wake Island raid on 5 October 1943. (National Archives 80-G-55338)

Curtiss built 135 SOC-1 floatplanes and 83 SOC-3s with interchangeable float/wheel landing gear, while the Naval Aircraft Factory produced 64 SON-1s (equivalent to the SOC-3). The three Coast Guard SOC-4s became SOC-3As when they were acquired by the Navy in 1942.

To train floatplane pilots the Navy ordered the N3N from the Naval Aircraft Factory in 1935, the first of these entering service in June 1936 as the N3N-1. After 179 aircraft had been completed, the NAF built 816 N3N-3s and both models served throughout WW II as primary trainers. A remarkably long career awaited the "Yellow Peril" as the last Navy examples were not retired until 1961.

By mid-1938 the Vought company had completed the prototype of an elegant monoplane that was to see a great deal of sea duty and become the most well-known floatplane of the war. This, the XOS2U-1 Kingfisher, shared initial production contracts with the SO3C, to meet a 1937 Navy requirement for an SOC replacement. The XOS2U-1 flew for the first time on 20 July 1938 and production models did supplant the SOC to a great extent, although not entirely.

The OS2U had in effect joined the Pacific Fleet on 16 August 1940 when the USS *Colorado* carried out trials with the new floatplane, which featured spot-welded fuselage construction for strength, an innovation at that time. The success of the test program led to the OS2U-1, fifty-five examples of which were built powered by a 450-hp P & W R-985 Wasp engine. Vought switched to the main production model, the OS2U-3, after completing 158 OS2U-2s, and built 1,006 examples before production was transferred to the Naval Aircraft Factory, which produced 330 examples under the designation OS2N-1 to round-out Kingfisher production at 1,550. Many served out their time as trainers.

Curtiss continued a long tradition of supplying aircraft to the fleet by developing the monoplane XSO3C as a successor to the SOC. But although the prototype flew for the first time on 6 October 1939, the SO3C required a lengthy development period before it was, with some reservations, deemed suitable for operations. Facing serious opposition from the OS2U which had been a success from the start, the Seamew failed to make the grade. Under-powered and unstable, it was never to be anywhere near as reliable as its older sister. As related above, it was withdrawn from shipboard service in 1944, and thereafter served as a landplane.

The war had entered its penultimate year before Curtiss again entered the picture with a floatplane that looked every inch a 'fantail fighter'. Sleek and almost twice as fast as any previous type, the SC-1 Seahawk broke with previous floatplane tradition by being designed as a single-seater.

This configuration was a reflection on the changing, indeed dwindling, role of the fixed-wing shipboard aircraft; and an answer to the relatively low survivability, due to modest performance, that hallmarked the SOC and OS2U. That said, the entire shipboard spotting role had always been something of a compromise; to do the job well, aircraft needed to carry the weight of a pilot and observer and be slow enough to make accurate assessment of results, particularly shelling.

Luckily, sustained opposition from enemy fighters rarely materialized to put out the long range eyes of the capital ships. What happened if slow and modestly-armed floatplanes were exposed to determined fighter attack was demonstrated during Operation TORCH and this was not the only time that observation

The designator "Fleet Air Photographic Squadron Atlantic 2" on this J2F-2A Duck indicates just one of the many roles handled by the capable Grumman amphibian which first flew in 1933. Another was rescue, as simulated in this mid-war view. (National Archives G/K 80-13772)

An OS2U-2 Kingfisher (BuAer 3102) in overall light gray and prewar national insignia, taxiing in a moderate swell during acceptance trials in Long Island Sound, October 1941. (Vought)

Not as good as the aircraft it was intended to replace aboard ships, the Curtiss SO3C Seagull/Seamew was prematurely retired and relegated to land bases. (US Navy 22821)

As the most powerful US floatplane to see war service, the Curtiss SC-1 served into the post-war era. This view shows BuAer 35299 on a "type recognition" photo sortie on 24 August 1944. (US Navy 448727)

planes came under aerial attack. Most floatplane losses in combat were due to the effects of ground or seaborne AA fire, however.

But not everyone agreed that to give shipboard aviators a "P-47 on floats" was the way to go, as the SC-1 required a completely new operational technique. In general though, pilots grew used to doing the job previously assigned to two crewmen and liked its good turn of speed to get them out of trouble in a hurry.

The first of 568 SC-1s and nine SC-2s accepted by the Navy were delivered to the *Alaska* Class battleship *Guam* on 22 October 1944. Working to redress its unfortunate experience with the SO3C, Curtiss came up trumps with the SC-1. Although room was made for a casualty occupying a litter in a fuselage compartment, the manufacturer eventually 'bowed to tradition' and modified the airframe to create the SC-2, a two-seater with a fully blown canopy, uprated engine and improved equipment. But the war was over before any reached the fleet, the last example not being delivered until October 1946.

The SC retains a place in US Naval history as the fastest floatplane to see shipboard service as well as the last of its class. In terms of top speed it came second only to the Spitfire Mk IX floatplane which remained an experimental type and was intended as a fighter rather than a shipboard aircraft.

Japan took an early world lead in high performance single-engined floatplane design and produced a number of aircraft with exceptionally clean lines. These were the Kawanishi N1K1 Kyofu (Rex) floatplane fighter, the Aichi M6A1 Seiran and Kawanishi E15K Shuin (Norm), built respectively for the attack and reconnaissance roles. Much use was made by the Japanese Navy of what might be termed the first of the fast combat floatplanes, the Mitsubishi A6M2-N (Rufe).

None bear too close a comparison with the SC-1 due to the differing roles but it is interesting to record that Curtiss almost accidentally produced what might have been a useful combat aircraft in its own right, had the US ever deployed floatplanes in the same way as the Japanese.

Radar reduced but did not remove the ongoing need for visual confirmation of Naval gunfire and as the war in the Pacific reached its crescendo this remained the primary task of shipboard floatplanes. Other duties tended to diminish; as hostile areas of ocean shrank in relation to Japanese defeats, so the use of floatplanes on ASR work also declined. With a high number of warships and submarines, plus Dumbo flying boats usually on hand to rescue aviators or sailors, the floatplane's requirement for the parent vessel to slow down for recovery (always an anxious time for many battleship and cruiser skippers) could be the least attractive option.

With victory in sight and new ships for the post-war fleet already in commission and on the nation's slipways, the vastly more versatile helicopter was awaiting its time even as the US fleet sailed triumphantly into Tokyo Bay in August 1945. The SC-1 soldiered on into the early years of peace but by the time American warships were engaged in another conflict off Korea, the floatplane era had passed into history.

This narrative concentrates exclusively on the use of the relevant aircraft types configured as floatplanes, rather than landplanes. All of them were operated extensively from land bases with wheels substituted for floats and many spent their entire service lives on training duties.

Thousands of routine tasks by millions of individuals contributed to the Allied victory in WW II, a con-

An experiment to expand the use of ships that carried floatplanes during WWII involved six *Fletcher* Class destroyers. Lengthy operational trials and some combat showed that the concept offered few advantages and the need to slow down to recover aircraft compromised the destroyers' role even more than it was perceived to do with larger ships. *Pringle* (DD-477) was photographed during trials with an OS2U-3 (BuAer 5315) off Charleston, SC during December 1942. (National Archives 80-G-20834)

flict so wide-ranging and so lengthy that there were inevitably a great many people whose duty went largely unnoticed by the general public. Although floatplane exploits did occasionally hit the headlines, few of these men felt like heroes, unsung or otherwise.

But some gave their lives in attempting to provide the fleet with vital long range information at a time when having an aircraft aloft could mean the difference between an ambush and an equal fight. And if the worst did happen, the entire aviation division, aircrew, maintenance personnel and catapult teams, often shared the fate of the rest of the ship's company. This book is therefore a modest attempt to give "floatmen" back some of the spotlight by sharing some of their first-hand experiences with a wider audience. If nothing else, theirs was a duty that was entirely unique.

Notes
I. The SO3C was originally going to be named Seagull after the SOC Seagull was replaced and although the British adopted the name Seamew for examples delivered under Lend Lease, this was never widely used by US forces. Only the type designation is used in this narrative to avoid any confusion.

2. Exact date unconfirmed.

Wooden ramp at an inshore patrol squadron station with depth-charge armed Kingfishers being readied for another sortie. As related in the text, some of these early wartime anti-sub operations were ad hoc, to say the least. (USCG)

1

ATLANTIC DEBUT

In the period of 1940-41, just short of war the US fleet was far from inactive; Germany's disregard of international agreements on the safe passage of neutral ships through waters patrolled by her U-boats, was demonstrated almost immediately after war broke out in Europe in September 1939. Consequently, US aircraft and ships assigned to patrol duties off America's Eastern seaboard and out into the Atlantic were put virtually on a war footing.

Much of the "Neutrality Patrol" duty fell on the shoulders of the men who crewed Coast Guard cutters and patrol planes – among them the SOC Seagull and J2F Duck. Their contribution to the wartime work of the service far outweighed the modest numbers of airplanes and ships available.

With a small surface fleet of cutters, some of which were adapted to embark a single J2F, the Coast Guard patrolled vast areas of ocean, from Greenland to Puerto Rico, Boston to Alaska. Coast Guardsmen also maintained the International Ice Patrol, rescued shipwrecked mariners and aviators and generally helped expedite the lawful passage of shipping.

After war was declared in Europe, Axis vessels were investigated and interned. To counter the acute risk that the Germans would attempt to establish radio and weather stations in Greenland to communicate with U-boats and aircraft, Coast Guard air and sea assets had an additional "early warning" task to prevent that dangerous possibility. The Navy took over the defense of Greenland in agreement with the Danish Government on 9 April 1941 and the Coast Guard became part of the Navy on 1 November 1941, an association that was to remain in force until 31 December 1945. The nine Coast Guard stations in operation in November 1941 were placed under the jurisdiction of the appropriate Naval District.

Coast Guard floatplane procurement included fourteen JF-2s in 1934 and ten J2F-5/6 models between 1942 and 1948. Three SOC-4s were acquired in 1938, these subsequently being taken over by the Navy and 53 OS2U-3s were delivered between 1942 and 1944. All these types were used on various in-shore patrol duties including vital anti-submarine searches - although these were at first, on very much an ad hoc basis. Radioman Robert L. Gregory began his career flying the SOC-4 and later the OS2U. He recalls:

"At Dinner Key, Miami, the officer of the day did the flight scheduling – there was no such thing as a briefing. The plane was fueled, loaded with

Elmer Stone, the first Coast Guard aviator, ready to board a J2F in full flying kit. The photo hatch used as an impromtu bomb bay by the cutter *Northland's* crew and related in the text, is clearly visible. (US Coast Guard)

bombs and a pilot was assigned to the flight. Each pilot flew what he thought was the correct altitude to observe a submarine and be able to attack it before it could damage any friendly ship in his patrol area.

"The aircraft radio transmitter was set on 300 kc, convoy frequency. To change frequencies, a coil had to be removed from the transmitter and changed – a task that generally required some skill.

"Our patrol area out of Miami was regularly south to a line drawn roughly from Key West out to Dog Rocks in the Bahamas, north of Cuba and as far east as Fort Pierce, Florida."

Wartime expansion of Coast Guard aviation reflected both the additional responsibility of AS patrol and a huge increase of shipping traffic into and out of US ports. While many Coast Guard personnel volunteered for the Navy, the fleet of small CG ships was maintained and increased. Included in wartime procurement were additional ships which embarked aircraft, such as the

The USCG cutter *Northland* with her J2F secured on the fantail adjacent to the ship's main battery. (USCG)

five 269-foot icebreakers of the *Wind* class. Each vessel carried a single floatplane or amphibian, the first one, *Northwind* (WAG-278), being launched in December 1942.

Older ships were armed and remodeled for war, among them the 216-foot cutter *Northland* (WPG-49), built in 1927. Modifications included installation of a boom and winch aft of the boat deck for hoisting a patrol plane aboard and an armament of two 3-inch and four 20-mm guns. *Northland*'s WW II duty was primarily that of maintaining a US presence in Greenland and a June 1944 patrol turned out to be quite eventful.

Lieutenant (j.g.) Ken Bilderbeck's service at the Coast Guard Air Station, Salem, Massachusetts from 1942 to 1945 included temporary duty with the *Northland*. On 2 June 1944, Bilderbeck flew J2F-5 BuAer 00775 from Salem to Casco Bay, Maine to provide the aviation element of the patrol along with his crew, ARM1c Spike Wojicki, AMM1c Frank Hoberg and AMM3c Sullivan Jones. The Duck was landed alongside the

Northland, hoisted aboard and secured for sea in a cradle near the ship's stern. The crew topped-off the tanks from a 50-gallon drum, 52 of which were lashed to the ship's deck rail.

Calling at St. John's, Newfoundland, Bluie West One in SW Greenland and Reykjavik, Iceland the *Northland* slowly plowed her way toward her northwest Greenland patrol area, having embarked army commandos at Reykjavik in mid-July. En route, gunnery practice on a suitable iceberg caused damage to the J2F. The Duck's tail overhung the *Northland's* aft 3-inch gun and the concussion stripped some of its wing, rudder and elevator fabric.

Repairs soon made the J2F fit to fly the first of many reconnaissance sorties and helping to plot a safe passage through the pack ice, the aircraft using the TBS "Talk Between Ships" VHF radio link to communicate with the *Northland*. An abandoned German weather station off the Northeast Coast of Greenland was destroyed by the commandos to prevent any further usage by the

Still in her wartime camouflage the Coast Guard cutter *Storis* was busy pumping oil ashore to the weather station at Skjoldungen, on 24 September 1945. Her J2F-5 Duck has "H"-shaped wooden anti-gust locks securing the vertical and horizontal tail surfaces, and curiously, both wings have been removed and stowed. (USCG)

enemy. A German trawler was also sighted, actually on the ice. Abandoned and scuttled, it had become wedged in the ice and had popped up when the floes moved together.

Fog halted the *Northland's* progress for three days while the crew watched movies and tried to forget about home and women . . . then another trawler was sighted. The ship gave chase and sighted a German patrol plane flying in the direction of Dove Bay.

Suddenly, the *Northland* was rocked by an explosion, then another. Submarines firing torpedoes in pack ice was unheard of and as the ship's sonar was secured against ice damage, it was assumed that the trawler had sowed mines. After a five hour, full speed pursuit, the *Northland* overhauled the German trawler (the *Kehdingen*). Shots had been fired to discourage the crew rather than damage the vessel, which might have yielded valuable information on German activity in the area.

When the two vessels came into open water off Koldeway Island, the Americans found the entrance to Dove Bay icebound. The Germans were trapped. Three lifeboats soon stood out from the *Kehdingen* and the *Northland's* crew prepared to board. But the wily enemy had set demolition charges and the trawler quickly sank. The German crew were taken aboard the *Northland*.

Then came confirmation that the trawler had indeed had an escort. Lookouts spotted the conning tower of U-703, a Type VIIC boat. After a few rounds from the *Northland's* gun the U-boat began to dive and frantic efforts were made to ready the J2F for an attack. Two 200-lb demolition bombs were slung under its wings and at the first stretch of open water, it was hoisted over the side. Bilderbeck gave it the gun in barely enough water for a safe take off.

Climbing to 1,000 feet the Duck began an hour's fruitless search for the elusive submarine. The *Northland* was now in an "L" shaped stretch of water formed by creeping ice. The Duck was side-slipped in to splash down, taxi up and finish with a semi-controlled water loop, picking its way through broken ice before being safely hauled aboard.

Next day the search was resumed. Bilderbeck flew the J2F, with Lieutenant (j.g.) Tom Bright manning the camera while Ensign Walt Bartlett worked the radio. At 1,500 feet an expanding square search was initiated and an hour and twenty minutes later the U-boat was found on the surface.

The J2F's two dive-bomb attacks appeared to score a near miss on the vessel's stern but there was no answering fire from the submarine. Instead it quickly changed course and dived. Ken Bilderbeck takes up the story:

"The Duck had many great qualities but dive bombing was not among them. As we were flying twenty miles back to the *Northland*, I thought that

Equally at home among arctic ice floes or Pacific swells the J2F proved a highly useful aircraft to the US services throughout the war. This is almost certainly the J2F-5 carried by the *Storis*. (USCG)

what we really needed to attack this submarine was a depth charge. The idea of somehow using one of the ship's Mk VI depth charges kept flitting through my mind."

Back on board, the diameter of the Mk VI charge and the size of the Duck's camera hatch, located in the center of the hull below the radio compartment, were compared. It fitted with inches to spare. Lines slung over part of the aircraft structure below the radioman's seat supported the charge.

"The plan was to lower the charge after we became airborne and then drop it by cutting the line. The Bureau of Aeronautics would have shuddered, to put it mildly, at this lashup."

The Duck duly took off with the Mk VI charge attached. The *Northland* aircraft was joined in the search by another Coast Guard J2F, piloted by Lieutenant (j.g.) Paul Hersey from the cutter *Storis*. Two and a half hours passed. No sub.

Bilderbeck obtained permission to jettison the depth charge in the planned way. It exploded in a suitably impressive column of water and ice and the Duck crew felt that their makeshift bomb would have worked "in anger" if the U-boat had been found. It never was.

The *Northland* transferred its prisoners to the CG cutter *East Wind* and continued on patrol until early October when the arctic nights began to draw in. The J2F was put ashore and Ken Bilderbeck went home. *Northland* continued her patrol work until her decommissioning in March 1946.

Three days after Pearl Harbor, on 10 December 1941, the USS *Brooklyn* took part in the operation to secure the island of Martinque. During the otherwise peaceful occupation, one of her floatplanes attacked a U-boat. The vessel was claimed as sunk by the SOC's small bombs, but the submarine was merely obliged to dive and lived to fight another day.

American capital ships were to see a great deal of service in the Atlantic throughout the war and their scoutplanes were to become a familiar and comforting sight to crews of slow merchant ships plying the increasingly dangerous waters that lay between the North American continent and their destination ports in Europe.

Inshore Marines

Floatplanes were put to good use by Marine Corps inshore patrol squadrons although the early war period was also marked, as Richard M. Seamon remembers, by "interminable anti-sub patrols." Seamon spent six months assigned to VMS-3 during 1942, flying the J2F out of the Virgin Islands where the unit remained until decommissioning in May 1944.

"Even though the base commander, Colonel (later General) Ford "Tex" Rogers would not allow landing lights on the runway (it was actually more of a polo field) lest a German sub surface and shell us, we were quite sure that enemy sub commanders knew the limits of our patrol area and stayed outside it to torpedo merchant ships at will.

"To my knowledge we never had the opportunity to attack a German sub – which was probably just as well since our 100-lb and 250-lb depth charges were rather puny. Occasionally we were able to locate lifeboats filled with survivors from torpedoed ships and direct them to the nearest land. Once when some badly shot-up survivors came ashore on

Marine Scouting Squadron Three and other units were issued with J2Fs to give the Corps a useful patrol capability from far-flug overseas base during the war. These VMS-3 aircraft are in Neutrality Patrol markings with unit designators including the "A" suffix denoting aircraft armed with guns and bomb racks. (USMC via Dick Seamon)

The cruiser *Indianapolis* carrying three SOCs still in their pre-war Neutrality Patrol markings, including number 15 from Cruiser Scouting Squadron 4, despite the wartime date of April 1942. The starboard catapult was removed under a late-war refit program. (Floating Drydock CA-35-2)

a small uninhabited island, Maj. Edward Carney and I flew out and made a water landing to pick up a badly burned seaman. He unfortunately died a few days after we brought him back to St. Thomas in the J2F.

"What I remember most about the J2F was its surprising agility that belied its obviously rugged construction. We had no hesitation in rolling it onto its back or making practice dive bombing runs and we occasionally broke the monotony with impromptu aerobatics – loops, chandelles and so on – even though we had bombs or depth charges hanging from the wings.

"As for its ruggedness I can report with some reminiscent embarrassment that one night, when there was nothing but a signalman with a search-light at the downwind end of the short runway, I failed to correct properly for the constant crosswind that we coped with almost automatically during daylight. I drifted into the side of a hill. Bombs were flung across the field, a wheel was driven up into a wing and my head made a dent in the windshield. Only that tough Grumman construction saved me.

"Then there was the time that we sent two J2Fs to San Juan, Puerto Rico for a week to escort ships in and out of the harbor. This was apparently due to a Navy squadron having difficulty keeping its PBYs flying. The runway at Isla Grande Field was, like so many airfields, continually under construction and there was a sharp drop of a few feet where the concrete ended on the downwind edge.

A Coast Guard OS2U-3 armed with depth charges on a wartime inshore patrol. This version of the Kingfisher represented the most numerous floatplane type operated by the Guard during hostilities, a total of 53 being acquired. (USCG 1653)

"Returning from a pre-dawn patrol, one of our pilots, determined to make as short a landing as possible, set his plane down and was startled to find he had no brakes. Then he looked over the side and discovered he had no wheels. He had come in a bit too short and sheered off both wheels on that ridge of concrete. The reliable, tough old J2F of course, slid sedately to a stop on its big float and was soon repaired."

Navy floatplane crews shared the uncertainty that war brought. Paul D. Keough had made Radioman Third before he flew a few times in the OS2U-2 out of Floyd Bennet NAS although the Navy had not yet established a separate rating for aviation radiomen.

The missions flown by the resident unit, VS-1D3, were anti-submarine patrols at sunrise and sunset in the coastal waters off New York and New Jersey, generally of four-hour duration at an altitude of 1,000 to 2,000 feet.

"By the time of my first flight in an OS2U, several months had passed since equipment familiarization at school. Nobody seemed concerned about this. There was no checkout as to whether I was qualified to operate the radio or knew the basics required of an airplane crew member. And whether I attached the parachute or the safety harness correctly to myself is still doubtful in my mind . . . possibly this overall attitude may have prevailed because radio silence was normally imposed and thus there was no expectation that equipment familiarization would be a real requirement.

"There was a .30 caliber machine gun to the rear of my seat. No ammunition was provided. I tried rotating it one time and could not figure out how to manipulate it."

After his short exposure to flying, Paul Keough transferred (with some relief) to destroyers.

Occasionally, Navy OS2U crews did sight U-boats and at least twice assisted naval units in sinking them. The first was U-576, a Type VIIC which had earlier attacked a convoy and sunk two ships. Sighted by two aircraft from VS-9 piloted by Ensigns Frank C. Lewis and Charles D. Webb on 15 July 1942 off Diamond Shoals, North Carolina, the Kingfishers shared the kill with the auxiliary vessel USS *Unicoi*, which rammed the U-boat under.

Almost a year passed before the next U-boat met its end in similar fashion when on 15 May 1943 U-176, a Type IXC, was spotted by an OS2U in the Nicholas Channel, off Cuba. The submarine was submerging and on the point of attacking a convoy when the floatplane dropped depth bombs and smoke pots to summon help. The Cuban subchaser CS.13 obtained a good sonar contact and destroyed the boat with depth charges.

A Coast Guard OS2U acting as a good shepherd to a convoy entering far from totally safe inshore US waters. The Guard's Kingfishers carried underwing depth charges to take care of U-boats. (USCG 1655)

2

EARLY PACIFIC OPERATIONS

The USS *California*, sunk at her pier in Pearl Harbor on 7 December 1941, still mounts one of her Kingfisher float planes, seemingly undamaged amid the carnage. (National Archives)

By the time the Japanese attacked Pearl Harbor on 7 December 1941 the OS2U Kingfisher had virtually replaced older type floatplanes on US battleships. And although some floatplanes were inevitably lost aboard those ships that were sunk or damaged and others were destroyed on Ford Island, a sufficient number of aircraft were already on Navy charge elsewhere to provide replacements.

Some bizarre incidents resulted from the Japanese attack. *West Virginia* had one of her two OS2Us blown clean off the ship although it is believed that this aircraft, apparently little damaged, was later repaired and put back into service. One of *Maryland's* OS2U-3s was not so fortunate. Although the parent ship suffered only minor damage, the catapult-mounted Kingfishers were highly exposed to flying steel, both Japanese and American. A hit wiped almost the entire OS2U airframe off the catapult, leaving only the main float.

Arizona went down with her two OS2U-3s but the crippled *California* had her OS2U-3s in place days after the attack and these particular machines may have subsequently been salvaged. The Kingfishers aboard the *Oklahoma* almost certainly were lost when the battleship sank.

One of the OS2U-2s assigned to the *Pennsylvania* and nicknamed "The Bug" was hurriedly patched up after the Japanese attack and launched on 8 December (Hawaiian time) to conduct a search for enemy fleet elements. None was found, but this particular Kingfisher (BuAer No 2201) was later involved in a headline-grabbing rescue operation that brought the humble floatplane to the attention of the American public.[1]

For the floatplane crews assigned to battleships and cruisers, WW II combat operations saw some changes. The prewar VO (Observation Squadrons) and VCS (Cruiser Scouting Squadrons) which had previously supplied aircraft and personnel to each ship, were replaced by a system whereby floatplane pilots and crewmen became part of the ship's company as the Aviation or "V" Division. New aircraft and when necessary, personnel, were assigned to ships on an "as required" basis for the duration of hostilities.

This did not mean that old squadron identities were entirely abandoned however, and indeed aircraft that previously had been assigned to observation and cruiser scouting squadrons continued to be identified as such in records and reports. The difference was that as the war progressed and combat took its inevitable toll, replacement personnel and aircraft were often drawn straight from training unit pools rather than squadrons.

Historically, the US Navy had placed great importance on the ability of its heavy and light cruisers to carry as many spotter aircraft as practicable and have adequate hanger and maintenance space. Prewar cruiser design, subject to treaty restrictions, international agreement and differing operational requirements, naturally led to considerable variation in configuration - number and arrangement of turrets, guns of different calibers, stack location and space allocation to aircraft. Up to seven aircraft were carried by some ships before the war, although the average number was between two and four.

Generally, in cruisers of both prewar and wartime construction, the aircraft catapults, cranes and floatplane stowage area were in one of three locations, depending on ship size and layout; (a.) amidships for both battlecruisers of the *Alaska* Class and the *Pensacola*, *Northampton* and *Portland* Classes of cruisers; (b.) aft of the stacks in the *Omaha* and *New Orleans* Classes and (c.) on the fantail in *Brooklyn*, *Wichita*, *Cleveland* and *Baltimore* Class ships.

It had been a prewar practice to place an aircraft catapult over No. 3 gun turret on some battleships, including *California*, *Maryland*, *Nevada*, *Oklahoma* and *Arizona* and this was not immediately changed when the survivors from Battleship Row were put back in the line. *Nevada*, the first to be repaired, sailed from Pearl on 19 April 1942 with her three OS2Us in place, two of them perched atop her No. 3 14-inch gun turret catapult. This catapult was generally removed during wartime refitting although some ships retained it for many months of war duty.

Available space aboard the older cruisers was often at a premium and this was one reason why the SOC was retained. Having the advantage of wing folding, the slow old biplane could be crammed into spaces that would not readily take more than two OS2Us, all models of which had non-folding wings.

Late-war replacement of the SOC and OS2U with the wing-folding SC-1 was implemented on cruisers but was not apparently, achieved in every case.

As the fantail had proved to be a safer and more spacious area in which to position catapults, aircraft cranes and hangers, all cruisers and battleships launched late in WW II or immediately afterward carried their floatplanes on the stern. Thus the postwar

Massive stanchions supported the midships catapults on the older classes of cruiser as demonstrated by the *Quincy* and her four SOCs in this 29 May 1942 New York Navy Yard view.(USN)

Much activity goes on while the catapult crew prepare SOCs for a sortie. The photograph was taken aboard an unidentified cruiser in January 1943. (National Archives 80-G 470115)

Fargo, Oregon City, Des Moines and *Worcester* Classes all featured fantail catapults at the time the ships were launched. No ships of the wartime *Oakland/Atlanta* Class, designed as anti-aircraft cruisers, carried aircraft.

First Encounter

When the Japanese struck Pearl Harbor, some cruisers were en route to the Hawaiian base, including *Northampton* (CA-26). She launched both her SOCs, BuAer Nos. 9951 (coded 5-CS-2) and 9934 (5-CS-4) at 1115 and the pilots, Lieutenant M. C. Reeves and Ensign F. H. Covington, soon realized that 7 December was a day unlike any other. Their task was to search for a distance of 150 miles to the northward of the ship's course. Approximately twenty minutes after launching the SOCs were fifteen miles west of Kauai when they were attacked by a fighter, identified as an A6M2 in the after-action report.[2]

The enemy aircraft made seven passes on the floatplanes, diving from above and from their side, following an initial "very fast" run from the port quarter. In response the SOCs adopted tight formation with the wingman stepped down, the section leader (Reeves) maintaining altitude at 300 feet, 80 kts ASI. Holding course until the A6M was in range, the SOCs then made an easy turn to port, putting their attacker on the quarter and allowing the free guns to bear.

When the Japanese pilot fired, the US gunners replied. The above maneuver was repeated every time the Zeke came in, the SOCs dropping low until they were just above the water and throttling back to lower their airspeed even further. On all diving attacks the enemy aircraft "presented an exceptionally good target as he squashed down toward the section . . . hits were seen during this type of recovery, particularly on the seventh and last attack. The Americans believed the Japanese pilot was unable to lead his target(s) sufficiently and observed that his attacks were "similar to those made by US Navy fighters during camera gunnery" .

Lieutenant Reeves' SOC received fourteen bullet holes, Ensign Covington's 11. Their respective gunners ARM1c R. Payter and ARM2c J. Melton, fired a combined 175 rounds, at least some of which evidently hit the Zeke, which was last seen leaving the area trailing smoke. The SOCs continued their search before proceeding to Pearl to have their damage patched, landing at 1527.[3]

Denying the Americans their naval "big guns" at the outset of hostilities was one of the Imperial Navy's most significant achievements on 7 December, for with the battleship force crippled at Pearl Harbor, the sea engagements of 1942 fell disproportionately heavily on cruisers. And although Japanese battleships were not heavily engaged during the period, her battlecruisers generally outgunned all but a few American vessels.

Floatplane pilots and crews therefore had additional responsibility in providing early warning that their parent ships were in imminent danger of attack. In the days when the early radar sets were limited in range and reliability, air searches became vital. When the Japanese ships demonstrated their prowess in night actions, the cruiser floatplanes dropped flares in an attempt to illuminate them.

It should perhaps be stressed here that in the event of the parent ship being sunk, it was not an en-

Bearing a telescope-weilding Donald Duck insignia on its fin, this OS2U almost certainly belonged to a shore rather than ship based unit. (USN)

tirely foregone conclusion that her observation aircraft would all be lost with her. It was logical, if there was time, to launch aircraft to seek a safe haven near land and on occasions this was achieved.

By late 1941, the existing US cruiser force had SOC-1s, -2s and -3s embarked, some ships carrying a mixture of Seagull models. Their first major test came in the Solomons and among the victims of the Battle of Savo Island was the *Vincennes*, on the night of 8/9 August 1942. Eye-witnesses stated that both the light cruiser's SOCs were in flames as she slipped beneath the waves.[4]

When the Solomons became the focal point of US attempts to curtail Japanese expansion, the waters around the notorious island chain became a graveyard for warships and transports as each side strove to consolidate slim gains. Almost nightly the "Tokyo Express" ran supplies and fresh troops down from the Home Islands via Rabaul and Truk, US sea and air forces doing their utmost to intercept and destroy these forces while maintaining and protecting their own supply runs.

At sea the US cruiser and destroyer force fought valiantly, the former frequently deploying their scoutplanes so as not to be caught unawares by any fresh moves by the Imperial Navy. While air searches were an undoubted advantage to ships that were otherwise blind, the crucible of combat also showed that floatplanes could represent something of a hazard. Having fully fueled and perhaps bombed-up floatplanes aboard did not constitute a very good insurance risk, should the parent cruiser come under enemy fire. If the

ship was too far away from a safe landbase where floatplanes could take refuge, more than one hard-pressed skipper had little choice but to dump them over the side. Accidents also took their toll, for almost everyone was new to this game.

During the preliminaries to the Battle of Cape Esperance (11-12 October 1942) *Salt Lake City*, *Boise*, *Helena* and *San Francisco* conducted air searches for Japanese ships. *Salt Lake City* lost one of her OS2Us to accidental ignition of flares stored in the fuselage and *Helena* had occasion to dump her aircraft.

This latter action was probably in line with criticism of earlier losses (especially at Savo) when gassed-up floatplanes and boats taking fire were perceived as contributory factors in the loss of the *Astoria*, *Quincy* and *Vincennes*. Concluding that a watch should have been set to jettison the floatplanes at the first sign of gunfire, Cominch (Admiral King) further decreed that airplanes should ride their catapults at night to facilitate this.[5]

This view tended to be enforced by the survival of *San Francisco* during the night Battle of Guadalcanal on 12-13 November. Having stripped airplanes and all other inflammable items from her hangar area, the ship suffered no peripheral fires. This is not to imply that airplane fires aboard cruisers were ever the direct cause of loss but at night, a blazing floatplane could act as a fine aiming point for enemy gunners who were more than adept at taking advantage of such help.

Battleships also found that scoutplanes could represent a hazard in combat. During a second night engagement south of Savo Island on 14-15 November, *South Dakota*'s after battery hit her own floatplanes on the fantail and ignited them. This potential danger was removed forthwith - another salvo simply blew the blazing OS2Us into the sea.[6]

This accident was criticized by Cinpac to the effect that the floatplanes should have been flown off prior to action. *South Dakota*'s skipper apparently had considered sending his aircraft to Tulagi but was unsure of what support facilities they would find there.

It can be seen that skippers whose responsibility was first and foremost to their ship and crew were occasionally faced with the dilemma of getting rid of their scoutplanes too early. On the other hand, once the enemy opened fire it could be too late to save them. In March 1943, *Salt Lake City* complied with Cominch's recommendation when she engaged a Japanese force that included three cruisers in the Battle of the Komandorski Islands. One of her OS2Us, ignited by Japanese fire, went over the side without causing any harm to the ship.

Floatplanes based at Tulagi supported further night actions; in the preliminary operations that led to the November 1942 Battle of Tassafaronga, newly arrived commander Rear Admiral Wright sent floatplanes from the heavy cruisers *Minneapolis*, *New Orleans*, *Northampton* and *Pensacola* plus light cruiser *Honolulu* to operate from Tulagi. A wise course in one way, this action was to prove negative due to unforeseen circumstances.

Although the latest Tokyo Express was surprised, the anticipated illumination of the enemy targets

The light cruiser *Concord* pictured on 10 November 1943 during flight operations at Hanga Roa, Easter Islands. The ship carried Admiral Byrd's base examination team which used a J2F named "The Galloping Ghost" for aerial survey work. (National Archives 80-G 2343)

did not materialize as the floatplanes had insufficient wind for them to lift off from the waters of Tulagi Harbor. Pilots tried for an hour and a quarter and when finally they did achieve flight, the battle was all but over. Tassafaronga was a minor disaster for the American team, *Northampton* being lost in return for one Japanese destroyer. And despite the floatplanes arriving late to drop flares, they could do little to affect the outcome.

Mercifully, the worst was over. After Tassafaronga the Japanese decided that trying to wrest control of the Solomons would only prolong a crippling attrition in men and ships which they could not afford. Plans were made to evacuate the remaining troops on Guadalcanal.

Training

One man who would have sympathized with the aviators' frustration at Tulagi was John A. Blaschke. Trained on the OS2U during the war, he went on to fly the SC-1 after hostilities had ceased. His Kingfisher time included some problems in making the beast fly:

"Comparing the SC to the OS2U (equates) to comparing a modern day high-powered Jaguar to an early model MG. All our training at Pensacola was in the OS2U, which was a very stable airplane, but a real clunker. It had marginal horsepower for take off, even under the best of conditions.

"On one occasion while I was still a cadet, I attempted to take off across the bay toward Santa Rosa Island. I never did get the OS2U in the air at full throttle and somewhat discouraged, taxied back, feeling guilty that there must have been something wrong with my technique. The ramp duty officer however, had some mechanics measure the propeller diameter.

"It turned out that OS2U propellers, which became badly corroded with saltwater after days and weeks of waterborne take offs, would develop pits and deformities in the tips. Each evening as they prepared the planes for the next day's flying, the mechanics would conscientiously file down these pits.

"What they didn't seem to realize was that this diligent 'maintenance' gradually eroded the length of the blades - and the propeller on the OS2U I had attempted to fly that day was approximately 10 inches shorter than the original prescribed length, and of course, could not provide enough power to get the aircraft into the air. When I was given another airplane, I was able to take off very rapidly."

When the cadet finally completed training and was assigned to a warship, that did not necessarily mean the end of his troubles. Freeman A. Flynn confesses that he felt like a rank beginner when he went to sea - and knew that many other pilots felt the same way.

An OS2U-1 from VO-1, USS *Arizona*, in October 1941 demonstrates the "Dog" method of underway engagement of the sled. The rating is about to make the hazardous trek forward to retrieve the hoisting sling. The aircraft is Bu/Aer 1696. (National Archives)

Flynn went through intermediate training and commissioning at Corpus Christi, graduated in July 1943 with about 250 hours of instruction and solo flying and waited six weeks in San Diego assigned to a service unit awaiting a ship. That turned out to be the battleship *Maryland* (BB-46).

"She was the first capital ship I ever saw or set foot on. There had been no operational training for me and the catapult and at-sea recovery system were complete mysteries, although there had been land-based catapults at Corpus Christi.

"I had trained in OS2Us in gunnery, glide bombing and over water navigation and was familiar with all these and other requirements, to the extent of about 100 hours in the aircraft but I knew nothing about gunnery spotting. This turned out to be the most important role we floatplane pilots had.

"From Pearl Harbor to the fall of 1943, the *Maryland* had had patrol and backup assignments that were very frustrating for the crew. Then came the Tarawa invasion in November 1943. *Maryland* was the command ship and as a rookie pilot my service involved patrol, scouting, photography and delivery of documents to other ships by air-drop. Our senior aviator and the pilot on the admiral's staff flew so low over the atoll that they came back with rifle bullet holes in both planes. They had to fly low to accu-

rately assess the situation during the first day's battle plan.

"Radioman Robert Houle, who subsequently flew primarily with me, received a Purple Heart for being wounded at Tarawa. He got another ten months later for flying support at Peleliu.

"In comparing flying qualities of the SOC and OS2U, both were about the same, with the latter being slightly faster and more maneuverable. Both were very rugged aircraft and our particular OS2Us took a lot of abuse. We went through about nine planes from October 1943 to February 1945 and as I recall, replacements were always available from forward area service units. But if necessary our crew could carry out repairs, even to the extent of refitting an OS2U's wing in Leyte Gulf!

"Of these nine planes, two were wrecked as a result of crane failure aboard ship, one during recovery. Both crewmen were saved without injury. Two aircraft were shot up enough to warrant replacement and two had a mid-air collision as a result of pilot error but due to superb flying skill both managed to get safely back to the *Maryland*.

"Two more were exchanged with a cruiser as we left Saipan en route to Hawaii for repairs after losing 45 feet of bow to a torpedo hit on 22 June 1944. During an earlier call at Pearl our ordnancemen had worked up a twin 30-mm gun mount for the rear cockpit of two of our OS2Us - of course these were the very planes we traded with the cruiser.

"For our newly rebuilt and well maintained aircraft we got a couple of tired, worn out OS2Us. Salt water corrosion had done its deadly work and the wing bolts were eaten almost one third through. I crossed my fingers on every catapult shot, praying that the wings would stay on. They did and we got replacements back at Pearl.

"It was the proliferation of carriers that changed the floatplanes' main scouting and anti-submarine patrol duty. Within a year and a half of my joining the *Maryland*, the primary function had changed to gunfire spotting. This along with sea rescue, was justification enough for retaining the OS2Us aboard ships, but represented a real reduction in activity nevertheless.

"Authorization for floatplane flights were part of battle plans in combat but when the ship was detached from fleet activities the captain authorized flights. The gunnery officer, navigator or captain would brief the senior aviator who would assign pilots. Two planes flew over target areas all the time the ship was on station for bombardment duty, one spotting gunfire while the second searched for targets. We took this duty in turn and changed roles during the bombardment.

"Tarawa experience, where the ship bombarded for a few hours, was lengthened to three full days at Peleliu. *Maryland* fired 1,550 rounds of 16-inch shells, mostly by two and four-shot salvoes with the secondary 5-inchers firing as many or more rounds. The ship came up in the water by it seemed, seven or eight feet after all that weight had gone!

"Floatplanes normally flew expanding square searches, starting from a known spot and continuing each leg to the limit of visibility, usually 12-15 miles in the Pacific. Anti-sub searches for example

Detail view of an OS2U being readied for a flight. Weathering of the main float and cowling is in evidence, as are strips of tape sealing panel joints under the fuselage and wing. The wing bomb/depth charge rack and the sled hook under the float can also be seen. (National Archives)

were usually about 4-5 hours duration. Our range was usually calculated in hours of fuel.

"Our crew on the *Maryland* included a catapult officer, several gunners, a crane operator, a chief boatswain and any number of men who handled the lines to the sled during recovery. The aviation unit had 16 men, all of whom except two had specialist ratings: two chief engine and airframe mechanics,

A January 1943 view of the stern of the *Alabama* shows an OS2U on the battleship's starboard cat. All guns are trained outboard to lessen risk of obstruction when the floatplane is launched. (National Archives)

20

three radiomen, an ordnance man, a parachute rigger and the services of the ship's photographer.

"We communicated with the *Maryland* directly by radio during spotting work, by flag signal when landing and light signals when in visual contact with our own or other ships. Light signals were efficient and kept use of the radio to a minimum, although with a radioman as crew we could always call up if there was the need. We had a wide band of frequencies and could call ships, fighter cover and so on.

"During floatplane recovery, that huge slick created by the ship turning 130 degrees through the wind was a godsend, although 30-foot swells could make the operation somewhat exciting. As I remember it, the recovery was often a source of fun and some pride in doing it well.

"I got to the stage of preferring the catapult launch to a water take-off. A cat shot was quick, positive, neat and clean. Any incidents were usually traced to pilot carelessness and in retrospect, funny. I once went off in pitch darkness and realized as I became airborne that I'd forgotten to ask the navigator where the target island was in relation to the ship. Another time (after some weeks of not flying) I neglected the checklist and lost my sunglasses to the slipstream. Having my head in an upturned position due to the force of the launch, my goggles flipped back over the headset and the chartboard slammed back to stop my right arm operating the stick properly - at 80 kts, six feet off the water!"

Lieutenant Commander Manny Blanco, who was assigned to the *Northampton* Class cruiser *Chester*, remembers that a vital part of an OS2U pilot's anatomy was the little finger of his left hand. The OS2U had a ring just ahead of where the throttle was in the "full power" position. That ring came in mighty handy during the catapult launch;

"The terrific forward thrust of the catapult sent arms, eyeballs and intestines surging backward. Hooking the little finger in that critical ring prevented the throttle from being retarded – a disastrous occurrence when the aircraft was so near the water."

Rickenbacker Rescued

Naval patrol squadrons, invariably equipped with the OS2U, were attached to land bases located around the US and overseas. Operating as landplanes where necessary, these Kingfishers were to equip 30 Naval District Inshore Patrol Squadrons prior to 1 March 1943 when they became Scouting Squadrons. (See Appendix 2)

When a B-17 Fortress ditched in the Pacific during October 1942 it was The Bug, the ex-*Pennsylvania* OS2U-2 then assigned to a unit based in the Ellice Islands that became part of the large scale search for survivors. Aboard the B-17 had been Captain Eddie V. Rickenbacker, W.W.I fighter ace and Medal of Honor winner. The search went on for three weeks until on 11 November The Bug found part of the bomber's crew. Flying the OS2U was Lieutenant (j.g.) F. E. Woodward, with ARM1c L. H. Boutte in the rear cockpit. Alighting near the downed bomber men, the Kingfisher crew spread yellow dye marker and began the rescue. Rickenbacker was still missing.

Then just before dark on 12 November this same OS2U found him. Flown on that occasion by Lieutenant

Recovering floatplanes could be a tricky business but the trailed sled to "catch" the aircraft taxying in the relatively calm "slick" caused by the parent ship turning was remarkably successful. An SOC is about to engage the sled alongside *Pensacola* in this view. (Ray Snapp)

An OS2U taking off from *Pensacola* during the bombardment of Wotje Atoll in the Marshalls in late 1943. (USN via Snapp)

William F. Eadie with Radioman Boutte again along for the ride, the Kingfisher touched down beside Rickenbacker's raft. As it was unable to fly with the weight of three extra men, Eadie decided to taxi his aircraft to the nearest land - 40 miles away. This feat was achieved with the most seriously injured B-17 crewman in the rear cockpit on Boutte's lap with Rickenbacker and another man riding lashed to the floatplane's wings. When news of this dramatic rescue was released the OS2U gained considerable fame. It would not be the last time that downed fliers were grateful to see a Kingfisher touch down.

Pensacola Diary

The war diary of the aviation unit aboard the heavy cruiser *Pensacola* (CA-24) is taken here as typical of many if not all cruisers as regards utilization of aircraft on war operations in the Pacific. It contains many items of interest relevant to this narrative and edited highlights follow.

From the establishment of aircraft aboard *Pensacola* in April 1930, some two months after her February commissioning until the outbreak of WW II, the aviation unit's function was scouting, reconnaissance patrols, spotting missions and training flights. Using two aircraft (SOCs by the outbreak of war) the unit had thus almost eleven years of training by the time of Pearl Harbor. Many hours were devoted to navigational flights, radio communications and surface spotting drills as well as anti-aircraft tracking for the ship's guns and towing sleeve targets for gunnery practice.

On 7 December 1941 the *Pensacola* was escorting a convoy to the Philippines and later that fateful month she positioned off Brisbane, Australia. On the 23rd, she catapulted an SOC-1 on a routine recon flight. Nothing more was heard from the airplane or its crew.

On 2 May 1942 two SOC-1s were launched, each carrying two 100-lb bombs to investigate any enemy activity on Howland and Baker Islands in the Gilbert and Ellice group prior to US occupation. Although they often carried bombs on spotting missions, this was the first and only time when *Pensacola*'s SOCs were launched solely to drop bombs. There was no need. The islands were deserted and the SOCs brought their bombs back.

After flying inner air anti-submarine patrols in support of the Solomons-Lae raid on 10 March 1942, *Pensacola*'s airplanes searched for downed flyers after the Battle of Midway that June. On 10 August the cruiser sailed for the Solomons, her SOCs carrying out routine searches until the 30th, when *Pensacola* took a torpedo hit in the Battle of Tassafaronga and was put out of action. She sailed for Pearl Harbor.

At Pearl *Pensacola*'s aircraft were detached to SOSU-1 and until the Fall of 1943, conducted training. When the cruiser was ready for sea again in November, her aviation unit received new aircraft in the form of OS2Us.

With the US on the offensive, *Pensacola*'s role was increasingly to be shore bombardment and on 19

November, she positioned off Tarawa. The OS2Us shared the spotting/anti-sub task and went on to support the Marshalls campaign, flying eleven sorties over Taroa and Wotje.

A spell with the North Pacific Fleet saw *Pensacola* in Alaska where the aviation unit shore-based at NAS Adak for routine patrols. The "hit and run" bombardment of Wake Island followed on 3 September, with Marcus Island and Iwo Jima also receiving high explosive "calling cards". In February 1945 cruiser planes flew twelve spotting missions in the Iwo operation and later, thirty-one missions supporting the occupation of Okinawa.

During the two phases of cruiser aircraft operation, what might be termed the "long range patrol" phase (up to 19 November 1943) and the "short range" phase to war's end, *Pensacola*'s aircraft stood by but were never actually required for air-sea rescue.

Among the difficulties associated with floatplane operations were recovery and maintenance. Recovery held the ever-present hazard of losing aircraft in rough seas and peripheral damage through the often precarious crane lift. OS2Us were criticized for their relative flimsiness and propensity for urgent repairs during bombardments. In that case the ship had little choice but to withdraw, which handicapped the troops ashore who wanted all the naval fire support they could get. *Pensacola*'s war diary states that this occurred "rather frequently" and at times, it was difficult to maintain all planes in operation, particularly, as at Iwo and Okinawa, when they were required to be in continual use.

Along with the Coast Guard, the Marine Corps was an early customer for the J2F Duck and all models were eventually operated, along with small numbers of OS2N-1s. The Marines acquired floatplanes for a variety of second-line duties but, obliged to defend a number of US-mandated islands likely to come under Japanese attack, the Corps was initially hard put to provide anything but a token force. Short of modern combat aircraft, it was forced to send floatplanes when something far more potent would have been preferred.

The island of Samoa was considered a probable target and the OS2Us of Navy Inshore Patrol Squadron VS-1D14 were dispatched there on 23 January 1942. These were followed by F4Fs and SBC-4 dive bombers. Fortunately, Samoa was not to share the fate of Wake Island or suffer the bombing that Midway received. On 22 April VS-1D14 was incorporated into Marine Aircraft Group 13; airplane strength was increased to seven OS2Us and two J2Fs, operated by eight officers and 68 enlisted men. Most significantly, this transfer was the first time that a Naval aviation unit had been attached to a Marine group. In May VS-1D14 was sent 100 miles northwest from Pago-Pago to Satapaula on Upolu Island in the British Samoas, there to join the 7th Marine Defense Battalion.

Even if the Japanese fleet never materialized, these outposts needed an American presence for reconnaissance and other duties, among them the provision of refueling points for ships and this duty fell to VS-2D14. A new OS2U unit, it was dispatched to Bora Bora, a literal dot in mid-Pacific where a cadre of seven VO/VCS pilots, including junior Ensign Larry Flint, set about establishing a fleet support unit assisted by 7,000 Army and Navy troops, plus the natives. The OS2Us were placed under Army command and the aviators initiated dawn and evening patrols, their aircraft each carrying two 325-lb depth charges, just in case anything was spotted. Hardly anything was and Larry Flint recalled refueling three ships in about eighteen months before the Bora Bora facility closed.[7]

Amphibian configuration was a primary reason for the Duck's development and ordering by the Navy for carrier on-board delivery duty. A J2F which appears to have a colored engine cowling, takes the wire on the CVE *Charger* in August 1942 while the deck crew prepare to guide a second machine in. (National Archives 80-G 14267)

A disabled, depth charge laden Grumman J2F (unit unknown) gets a tow from an Army crash boat off Oahu. Diamond Head is in the background. (Jay Groff)

Elsewhere in the Pacific, Marine Corps amphibian pilots found plenty of action and of all the unsung heroes of the bitter and bloody Solomons campaign, the small group of pilots who took it in turn to fly the single J2F Duck available for rescue work on Guadalcanal must come high on any list. From mid-1942, pilots were constantly on standby to pick up downed aircrew, among them Marine aviators Lieutenant Colonel Charles Fike and Major Joe Renner.

On 7 October, two more Ducks arrived and along with a solitary rescue boat, the efforts of the amphibians materily contributed to the overall low fatality rate among fighter pilots and scout/dive bomber crews shot down in the Solomons area. This was reflected in a ComSoPac commendation for Major Michael Sampas, who rescued no less than thirty-nine pilots and sixty-one crewmen and air-lifted 237 other persons to rear areas, in the space of three and a half months.[8]

There is only space here to outline floatplane rescue sorties, many of which were routine – but a few were made more hazardous through enemy action. On 7 June 1943, a big air battle developed over the Russell Islands and among the U.S. casualties was Lieutenant Samuel S. Logan of VMF-112. Logan's F4U Corsair was hit as he tried to rescue an RNZAF P-40 Kittyhawk pilot. He bailed out, only to be viciously attacked by a Japanese fighter which, having failed to shoot Logan in his parachute, then proceeded to try chopping the American up with his propeller. The flashing blades did hack off part of Logan's right foot and left heel, but another New Zealand Kittyhawk intervened to drive the Japanese fighter off. Logan landed in the sea and Lieutenant Colonel Nathaniel Clifford of MAG-21 flying one of the J2Fs, made the rescue.[9]

When the Japanese abandoned the Solomons sector of their outer defense perimeter, the reduction in air and surface actions made less call on rescue services. Floatplanes continued however to undertake patrol work and the late 1943 build-up of Allied airpower on Guadalcanal included six OS2Us for anti-submarine duties until such time as the Solomons were considered free of Japanese ships.

1. The Rickenbacker rescue - see later
2. The Japanese fighter's actual designation was not used in the original report - it was a little early in the Pacific war for such detail to be common knowledge. The actual description included the words: ". . . a single place fighter with enclosed cockpit (kept closed during entire engagement) . . . was of grayish or light khaki hue. The fuselage was marked by a wide red band. . ." Although the cruiser aviators astutely believed that the red fuselage band denoted a section leader - in this instance it actually identified an aircraft from the carrier *Akagi*.
3. USS *Northampton* After Action Report
4. Morison, S. E.: "History of United States Naval Operations in WW II"
5. Ibid
6. Ibid
7. Tillman, B.: "Where Are They Now" The Hook Summer 1988
8. Sherrod, R.: History of Marine Corps Aviation.
9. Ibid.

24

(Above) A Kingfisher spots the fall of shot from BB-57 *South Dakota* during a 30 January 1944 bombardment of Roi Namur, Kwajalein Atoll. (Joseph W. Butts)

(Below) An OS2U-3 from battleship *South Dakota* flown by Lt. Joe Butts with ARM 2c Moore probably in the rear seat.   (Joseph W. Butts)

3

HAZARDOUS BEACHES

Morocco

The importance of the November 1942 landings in North Africa to Allied inter-service cooperation could hardly be overestimated at the time. The invasion, composed largely of American troops, was the first step toward pushing the Germans out of occupied Europe. On its success or failure hinged the future of amphibious operations and its far-reaching effects would be to demonstrate to the world that the long-awaited "Second Front" in Western Europe was starting to be realized.

The Western Naval Task Force consisted of 102 warships, transports and auxiliaries, including the aircraft carrier *Ranger*, four CVEs, three battleships, three heavy and four light cruisers and nine destroyers. In total the BBs, CAs and CLs could launch a total of twenty-nine SOC spotters and four OS2Us. *Massachusetts* had lost one of her Kingfishers en route, the *Cleveland* (CL-55) being the only other ship then carrying OS2Us.[1]

As with the other Allied aircraft participating in Operation TORCH, the battleship and cruiser floatplanes had previously had their national insignia outlined with a wide yellow circle as an aid to recognition by friendly air and naval forces. Undoubtedly, it helped a little.

In the event, almost complete surprise was achieved by the invasion, which was divided into Southern, Center and Northern attack groups to assault the French Moroccan towns of Safi, Fedala and Mehdia respectively. In the confusion of the pre-dawn landings, French batteries at Fedala opened fire, drawing answering salvoes from *Brooklyn* and *Augusta*.

While the reaction of the Vichy French over airfields such as Port Lyautey gave Allied fighters little trouble, the naval observation planes were soon attacked by fighters and French flak. Enemy aircraft also flew sorties directly against US warships and *Massachusetts*, *Tuscaloosa* and *Wichita* responded quickly.

At Safi the landings were accomplished with little trouble. While the beachhead was being established *New York* and *Philadelphia*'s SOCs flew spotting missions for what little naval gunfire support was required. They also proved useful in conveying messages, the rear-seat observer dropping orders and other papers in sealed, waterproof bags.

French reaction in the air included strafing attacks by Dewoitine D. 520s of Flotille 1F beginning at

In an extraordinary confrontation between American manufactured aircraft, a Vichy French Curtiss Hawk 75, of the type shown here, downed one of the Vought OS2Us spotting for U.S. warships on 8 November 1942 near Casablanca. Both crewmen survived. (Lambert Collection)

0700 and these fighters attempted to drive away the SOC spotters. The French pilots apparently did not press the matter when the US floatplane gunners spiritedly blazed away at them![2]

One OS2U crew from *Massachusetts* were not so lucky. Set upon by Curtiss Hawks of GC II/5 based at Camp Cazes while patrolling near Ain Sebaa, the Kingfisher was damaged badly enough for it to be forced down. Pilot Lieutenant "Tommy" Dougherty made a water landing and taxied ashore. Both men were captured and gunner/observer Lieutenant Clyde Etheridge had his wounds, sustained in the combat, attended to in a French hospital.

Despite these mishaps the floatplanes' work was highly appreciated by Admiral Davidson who probably stirred the pot of inter-service rivalry by opting to have the SOCs from *New York* and *Philadelphia* perform close support rather than the F4Fs of the Santee air group. A number of these Wildcats had been wrecked in landing

A Curtiss SOC-3 of the Western Naval Task Force makes a low level pass over USS *Augusta* as the enlisted ARM throws out a message. (National Archives)

accidents at Safi airfield and the prudent floatplane crews appeared a more reliable alternative than young fighter pilots with more enthusiasm than experience.

As though to enforce the admiral's confidence, one of the cruiser floatplanes rounded out the day's operations by bombing the beached French submarine *Meduse* near Cap Blanco. It had been a disastrous Sunday for French forces.

The experience of the Northern Attack Group was far less satisfactory. Shore batteries added to the difficulties of the troops in securing the designated landing beaches and light cruiser *Savannah* was kept busy counter firing on the French coastal guns. *Texas* was prevented from using her 14-inch guns for fear of hitting American troops, but the battleship's SOCs joining with those from *Savannah* "made a potent contribution" in breaking up French tank columns coming up from Rabat by means of a novel but effective technique - dropping anti-submarine depth charges fitted with impact fuses. [3]

Against land targets, depth charges could be devastating. Their natural tendency to create shock waves in water set up a similar effect over hard ground to pound vehicles and tanks over an area many times that of conventional bombs. Troops were simultaneously assailed by fire, noise and sonic shock waves, the latter being enough to render men positioned anywhere near the detonation immediately unconscious if they were not killed outright. Thus the slow and relatively harmless SOC was quickly transformed into a deadly weapon.

Texas, her field of fire cleared, finally opened up with her main battery on the afternoon of 10 November. Lobbing 14-inch shells, the old battleship's guns scattered a French troop convoy on a road more than eight miles inland. [4]

Algeria

Concurrent with the landings in Morocco, an Eastern Naval Task Force sailed from England to put troops ashore at Algiers on 8 November. The largely unopposed landings near Oran, culminated in the formal surrender of all French units in Africa on 10 November.

Having totally lost the initiative in North Africa, Hitler moved swiftly to make any further Allied advance as costly as possible. German aircraft occupied Tunisian airfields and it took until the end of the year to contain the threat they posed and May 1943 before the Allies could proclaim the liberation of all North Africa.

Sicily

Operation HUSKY, the invasion of Sicily in July 1943, again saw strong US Naval elements supporting and protecting the landing force. Among the warships was the cruiser *Brooklyn*, whose floatplane pilots were to be thrown into the thick of the action, which included being intercepted by enemy fighters. Assigned to bombard Blue Beach off Monte Dususino, *Brooklyn* launched her SOCs in the early hours of 10 July 1943. While engaged in their gunfire spotting task, the floatplanes were attacked by Bf 109s, probably of Jagdgeschwader 53. [5] One of the cruiser floatplanes was badly shot up by a Messerschmitt pilot who correctly judged the degree of deflection necessary to hit the much slower biplane. The SOC nevertheless survived to stagger back to its parent ship, only to be further harassed by "friendly" Navy fire.

A second SOC had a crewman "shot out" by US fire and he unfortunately drowned. The cruiser floatplanes gamely continued their task without fighter protection, this lack being one of the unfortunate aspects of an otherwise successful landing operation. By 0945 troops were firmly on the beach and *Brooklyn* ceased firing. There were no targets left.

Marauding Messerschmitts also attacked SOCs from *Boise* and *Savannah*, which were part of the support for Dime Force off Gela. Both cruisers launched four SOCs to report on bombardment results. Bf 109s from Gerbini airfield drove them off, enemy fire killing Lieutenant Charles A. Anderson, *Savannah's* senior aviator. His radioman Ed J. True, was rescued along with Lieutenant (jg) George Pinto and his observer by the destroyer *Ludlow*. Seeing Anderson's SOC crash, Pinto landed nearby to render any assistance but his aircraft sank soon afterwards. After picking up the three aviators from a life raft, the destroyer sank the remaining SOC with gunfire.

Savannah launched two more SOCs at 0827, to find the Bf 109s waiting. One piloted by Lieutenant Osborn was shot down and the other fled back to the relatively safe protection of the fleet's AA guns to be recovered aboard at 1027.

Despite the casualties, naval commanders had little choice but to send the observation planes off as long as there was a need. It was vital to have up to the minute reports on any German positions that had been overlooked, the movement of reinforcements into the beachhead and the accuracy of shelling.

Flying from *Boise* the ship's senior aviator, Lieutenant Cyril G. Lewis, spotted for targets in company with the SOC flown by Lieutenant Harding. At around 0830 German tanks were seen on a coast road south of Niscemi. Passing coordinates to his ship, Lewis came under fire from the vehicles and the floatplanes were then attacked by two Bf 109Fs. The German pilots missed and failed to press the attack and short of fuel, Lewis headed back to the *Boise*.

Lieutenant Harding continued spotting the tanks and some results were observed as a result of the shelling but the presence of enemy fighters prevented the SOCs from completing their task. En route back to the *Boise*, Harding came under fire from the same Bf 109s that had shot down one of *Savannah's* SOCs.

Ensign Kalb Roher who had been catapulted from *Boise* to relieve Lewis over the target area, had to return with an inoperative radio but not before he had reported 15 more tanks and dropped his bombs. Lewis was launched again at 1215. He found the tanks, passed coordinates and saw three *Boise* salvoes strike home before glancing behind him to see two 109s diving. Three times the German pilots tried to nail the SOC and although their fire struck home, Lewis was unhurt.

The Gela assault force had other targets for naval guns and some troublesome shore batteries were pounded by *Savannah* for some hours. During the search for enemy guns, Lieutenant Osborn's SOC was shot down and the ship's remaining aircraft had returned

On average, it took about 23 lbs. of explosive rammed into a catapult charge, a casing shaped much like a .5-inch shell, to launch a floatplane from a battleship or cruiser. Here, an *Astoria* Class cruiser crew has just performed the task for an SOC in what Naval Historian Samuel Eliot Morison termed, "one of the finest sights in the modern Navy." (Emil Buehler Naval Aviation Library)

An SOC at the "moment of truth"; it did happen that at this point some aircraft failed to gain flying speed and were lost when pilot recovery proved impossible. Note the fully down top mainplane flaps as "No. 6" grabs the air. (Author's collection)

with damage. *Boise* continued to duel with the tanks which were increasingly threatening the beachhead. At 1102 *Savannah* was ordered to support *Boise* in stopping the advancing armor as well as maintaining counter fire on the shore batteries.

By 1205 the gun batteries fell silent and at 1219 *Boise* launched her planes to report the latest situation, the *Savannah* noting that, "The *Boise* and ourselves have lost all but one of our planes." An hour later the last *Boise* SOC was downed, reportedly by a Bf 109, after pin-pointing more tanks. The ship continued to fire on them until around 1300.

All day the ships kept up the rain of fire on the beachhead area, the Germans offering strong resistance to the invading Allied troops. But with American tanks finally ashore, the attack was contained although the battle raged well into the night. *Boise* and *Savannah* finally set course for Algiers on 14 July.

Over at Scogliiti, Center Force's four SOC spotters from *Philadelphia* were also attacked by Bf 109s. Having launched at 0530 the floatplane crews had a busy day. Three knock-out bombardments of enemy guns had been completed by 0715 although the SOCs were detected by the German fighters even in the half-light of dawn. One was shot down and the crew killed and *Philadelphia* was to lose two more SOCs before the day was out.

Lieutenant (j.g.) Paul Coughlin and Radioman 2nd Richard Shafer flew a spectacular and unusual patrol. Sweeping over the beach at Point della Camerina the SOC bombed and strafed enemy positions, whereupon white flags were seen. The Italian defenders seemed keen to surrender to this display of Allied airpower and Coughlin and Shafer obliged them, waving them toward the beach and capture. Riding herd,

the floatmen urged their prisoners on with bursts of gunfire until the group exceeded 100 men.

Attacked by 109s, the SOC escaped with the help of five-inch salvoes from their ship. Their prisoners had meanwhile scattered and gone into hiding but a few potshots at likely buildings brought them all out again and the SOC completed the capture. It was estimated that 150 prisoners had been taken for the expenditure of 1,000 rounds of .30-cal ammunition.

Italy

For USS *Savannah* Operation AVALANCHE, the September 1943 invasion of Italy, was a continuation of an intense period of European operations. Sicily had been followed by a number of shore bombardment sorties and, her SOCs replaced, the cruiser was available for the assault on Salerno. *Boise*, temporarily diverted from the main landings, beached her floatplanes to allow stowage of vehicles for a concurrent unopposed capture of Taranto on 8 September. She then left to join *Brooklyn*, *Savannah* and *Philadelphia* in the Southern Attack Force for Salerno.

As the troops battled their way ashore on 9 September there was no immediate help from the fleet. Due to a belief that the landings would, after the Italian surrender, be unopposed, there was no pre-invasion naval bombardment. The Germans had meantime fortified the beachhead area; but a foothold was secured on D-Day and at 0914 *Savannah*'s first salvoes were on their way, her SOCs spotting for the guns in company with Army A-36 Invaders. Shortly afterwards flagship *Philadelphia* opened fire to begin a ten-day operational stint off Salerno, pounding enemy batteries, troop positions and tanks, likewise pinpointed by her SOCs.[6]

Savannah was hit by a radio-controlled bomb on D-plus two, 11 September, and damaged badly enough for her to withdraw to Malta. *Boise* replaced her although the cruiser was, like many Allied ships, hampered by the confusion of a heavily contested landing and a lack of shore fire-control parties. Much of the action took place at night which prevented the use of spotter planes and even during daylight, the SOC crews faced great difficulty in positively identifying enemy and Allied positions.

Nevertheless, the contribution of the US cruisers was invaluable to ultimate Allied success at Salerno, the operation being concluded by mid-October. A tougher test for the ground forces lay ahead, at Anzio. Few calls for heavy gunfire support were requested during the early phases of Operation SHINGLE although *Brooklyn* was in action on D plus one, 23 January 1944, adding her gunfire support to the struggle to clear the beaches.

On 8 February *Philadelphia* relieved *Brooklyn*, her own action period ending on 12 March when she sailed for Naples where many of the US ships were home-ported. Both cruisers joined forces to support the final troop breakout in May. SOCs spotted for the ships' guns at Gaeta where enemy batteries were located. *Philadelphia* collided with the destroyer *Laub* and had to withdraw to Malta for repairs while *Brooklyn* conducted two days of bombardment to close out the American cruisers' part in the campaign. Rome was liberated on 5 June, by which time the US cruisers were in British waters, preparing for an amphibious operation of even greater magnitude.

Northern France

For Operation OVERLORD, the invasion of Normandy on 6 June 1944, capital ships of the US Atlantic Fleet were an integral part of the vast Allied naval armada. They were battleships *Arkansas*, *Nevada* and *Texas* and cruisers *Augusta* (flagship, Western Naval Task Force), *Tuscaloosa* and *Quincy*.

Although German targets in the Normandy area had been all but neutralized, reaction by the Luftwaffe could not be entirely ruled out. Allied air supremacy was almost guaranteed but it was decided – with the experience of TORCH operations still fresh – not to risk the US warships' OS2Us and SOCs to spot for their parent ships in the initial bombardment. Instead, the floatplane pilots were given the little publicized role of being among the first US flyers over the historic beachhead – but in aircraft far better able to defend themselves than their usual mounts, namely Spitfire Mk Vs.

So it was that Lee-on-Solent airfield in Hampshire witnessed an unusual gathering of American battleship and cruiser floatplanes early in June. The aircraft were brought ashore and secured against bad weather

SOCs and OS2Us secured against the English weather as NAS Lee-on-Solent in June 1944. Brought ashore from Atlantic Fleet ships engaged off Normandy and Southern France, the US floatplane spotter pilots temporarily switched to Spitfires for the duration of the Allied landings. (National Archives 80-G-302116)

while their pilots went off to fly British fighters. VOS-7[7] had newly formed for this unique operation, with 17 aviators from the three battleships and three cruisers flying sorties as part of an Air Spotting Pool known as No. 34 Reconnaissance Wing, Fleet Air Arm. Commanding the American detachment was Lieutenant Commander William Denton, Jr., the pilots including Robert Doyle and John Mudge.

Between 6 and 26 June VOS-7 pilots flew a total 209 sorties in the face of German flak and fighter attack, one Spitfire being lost. By the 25th, American ships were heavily shelling the French coast in support of the drive to take the vital port of Cherbourg, utilizing both their own floatplanes and the British fighters as spotters. Unfortunately, while the Germans had been forced to concentrate on advancing Allied troops and the naval bombardment, their flak remained deadly and among the airborne casualties was an OS2U which was shot down that day. With Cherbourg secured on the 26th, VOS-7's brief existence ended and the unit was disestablished.[8] Before the next major operation requiring gunfire support, the US capital ships had reclaimed all their spotter planes previously beached in England.

Southern France

The invasion of Southern France in August 1944, codenamed Operation DRAGOON, saw the deployment of *Arkansas, Nevada* and *Texas* plus *Augusta, Brooklyn, Marblehead, Philadelphia, Quincy* and *Tuscaloosa*, with *Cincinnati* and *Omaha* in reserve. Following night landings in Provence on 14 August the main force prepared to get ashore the following day and from 0730 the assault force ships laid down a heavy barrage of fire on German defenses. Spotting was carried out by

SOCs from *Brooklyn, Philadelphia* and *Quincy*, the work of the latter ship's aviation unit winning special praise from Rear Admiral Mansfield, RN in command of the gunfire support group composed of British and US ships. He signaled:

"I was particularly happy to have Captain Senn and his fine ship *Quincy* under my command . . . I wish especially to record the fine work done by her aircraft, both as spotting planes and also on reconnaissance sorties when information was lacking."[9]

In an operation that found far lighter German resistance than was the case in Normandy, DRAGOON lasted until 2 September, it being concluded more quickly than had been anticipated. Naval gunfire support was provided throughout the landings and despite the availability of a more specialized spotting force in the form of VOF-1's fighters, the capital ships generally preferred their own SOCs for this work. Thereafter the US Navy played only a minor part in the liberation of Europe – for the focus was now primarily the Pacific and final victory over the Japanese.

Notes:
1. The mix of floatplanes was the result of the failure of the SO3C – which the TORCH capital ships would otherwise have carried in this operation.
2. Shores, C.F.: Fighters Over Tunisia; Neville Spearman, 1975.
3. Morison, S.E.: History of U.S. Naval Operations in WW II.
4. Ibid.
5. Gruppen of JG 53 and JG 77 were among the German fighter units moved rapidly across North Africa to counter the TORCH landings.
6. Morison, S.E.: History of U.S. Naval Operations in WW II. Vol IX.
7. Some references state that this unit may have been designated VCS-7.
8. Mersky, Cmdr. P.: Naval Aviators in Spitfires – U.S. Naval Institute Proceedings, Dec 86.
9. Morison, S.E.: History of U.S. Naval Operations in WW II, Vol. IX.

Although the SO3C had a number of useful features for shipboard spotter plane use including full wing folding and the Curtiss "turtle deck" rear fuselage, it was unstable and under-powered. An inshore launch is being made from the cruiser *Boston* in this view. (National Archives 80-G-378898)

4

BRING 'EM BACK ALIVE!

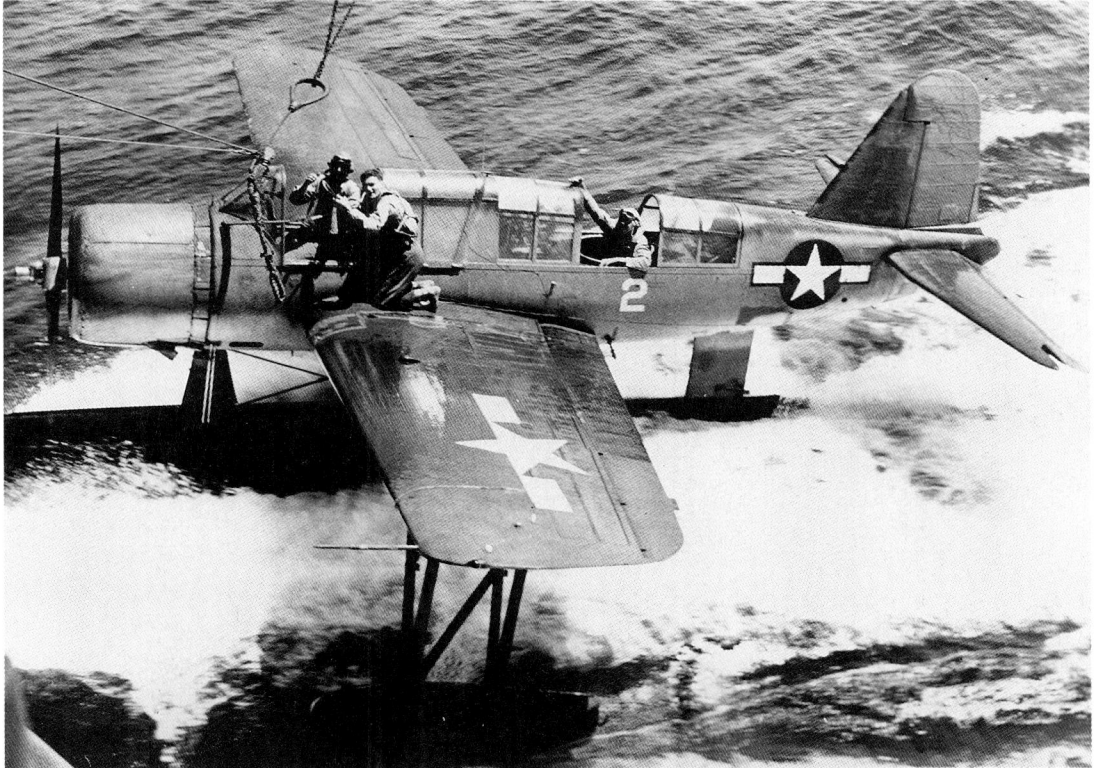

Almost all fleet operations, including carrier strikes, involved battleship and cruiser floatplanes for rescue work. On 21 April 1944 one of *Boston's* OS2Us brought back a TBF crewman following carrier raids on targets in the Hollandia area of New Guinea. (National Archives 80-G-283564)

In January 1944 the Navy had accepted the last of 794 SO3C Seamews [1] and by March, the manufacturer had called it a day. To spend more money and effort in overcoming the SO3C's ills was simply not worth it, for the aircraft was chronically under-powered and had been unable to offer any great advantage, even over the ten year old SOC. Indeed, the Navy was glad to see the back of the few that made it aboard ships and none in fact survived beyond December 1943 in this role.

The story goes that Admiral Halsey took a personal hand in the demise of the SO3C by sending a dispatch to BuAer to have OS2Us as replacements, forthwith. The upshot of this order was that catapult crews were offered the chance to be rid of the beast once and for all. The SO3Cs were positioned on the cats, which were primed and fired.

Jack A. Weber was a wartime Coast Guardsman who believes that the above order to relinquish the SO3C led to the Guard being asked to turn its OS2U-3s over to the Navy. In return the Coast Guard could have as many SO3Cs as it wanted. How the service viewed this trade can be summed up by Weber:

"At Floyd Bennett NAS, Coast Guard tests of the SO3C included a full-stall landing in sheltered

water in Rockaway Bay. When the aircraft touched down in full stall condition, the engine just snapped off and sank! This is the only time I recall the floatplane version being flown; it was a bad design, under-powered and a virtual monster to fly. The pilots hated it with a passion."

With the demise of the SO3C as a floatplane the US fleet standardized on the OS2U and SOC. The Navy's General Board believed that ships equipped with catapults should continue to operate spotter planes, despite some calls for their removal and replacement by increased armament. As the Pacific war gained momentum with the chance of major US defeats at sea receding, shipborne floatplanes demonstrated their usefulness on numerous occasions.

Outlying islands and territories which had by mid-1944 been liberated by US forces with Japanese counter attacks only a remote possibility, still needed guarding and air patrols remained vital. In such areas floatplanes could maintain a security presence without the need to tie down first line combat units needed elsewhere. The Aleutians and Alaska represented such a theater of operations and the J2F and OS2U were utilized there. Among its other duties the Kingfisher un-

A J2F showing the crane hook, the wire loop for which was stowed under a hatch in the aircraft's top wing center section. Ensuring a good "hook" could be quite demanding in a heavy ocean swell. (USCG Photo No. 44)

dertook an important air ambulance role and at NAS Kodiak some were operated with their rear cockpit armament removed to make way for a removable regulation basket stretcher.

Meanwhile as the Pacific air war intensified, so the need for the rescue of downed aviators increased. Following an 18 February 1944 carrier air strike on the Japanese base at Truk, an OS2U launched from the *Baltimore* to rescue an F6F pilot who was, "down in the drink". The Kingfisher, piloted by Lieutenant (j.g.) Denver Baxter with Reuben Hickman in the rear seat, spotted the Mae West. A water landing soon had Lieutenant George Blair of *Essex'* VF-9 perched on Hickman's lap.

As the floatplane approached the cruiser, Baxter voiced doubts that they would make it. So much gas

had been used hauling the extra weight that fuel was now dangerously low. But the pick-up was successfully made and when the OS2U's tanks were checked they contained little more than fumes . . .

Truk was to be the scene of an even more dramatic rescue in April. The duty of retrieving shot-down aviators was assigned to the *North Carolina* which alerted two OS2U crews on 30 April following the opening attacks the previous day.

Lieutenant Dowdle and Radioman Hill were alerted for the first morning rescue when Lieutenant Bob Kanze's Hellcat (VF-10) ditched south of the atoll. The OS2U taxied through rough water to reach him but as Kanze attempted to clamber aboard, a wave tipped the Kingfisher over. Lieutenants John Burns and Aubrey Gill

Keeping an eye on proceedings above Angaur, Palau Islands, one of *Portland's* OS2U-3s circles to radio any necessary corrections in the fleet's gunnery while the invasion fleet sails in, on 17 September 1944. Fully aware of what the little scoutplanes were up to, the Japanese invariably attempted to shoot them down, fortunately with only a modest success rate. (USN 283751)

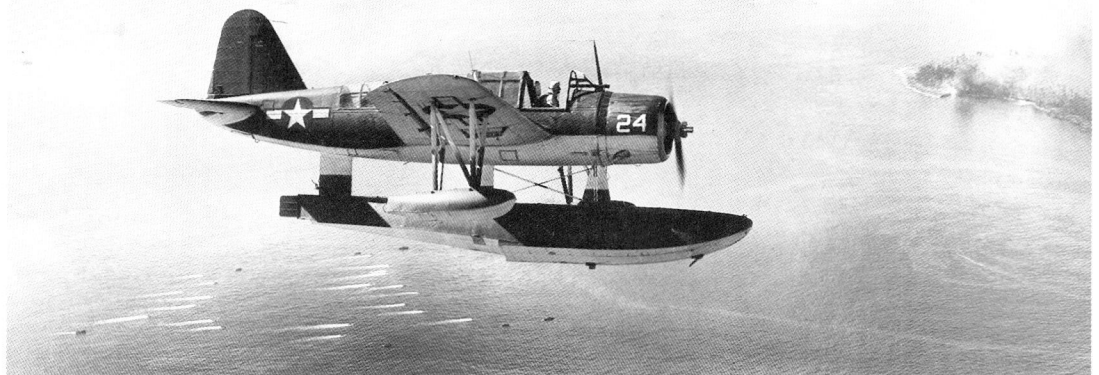

The entire Vought OS2U aviation detachment of BB-57, *South Dakota*, is photographed in flight by a Kingfisher from BB-60, *Alabama*. (Joseph W. Butts)

in the second OS2U circled the three men now hanging onto their life raft. Burns touched down and soon had Kanze and Dowdle lying on the wings, with Hill holding onto the fuselage.

There was no way now that the Kingfisher could take off and Burns taxied over to the submarine *Tang* which was in the vicinity on rescue duty. Burns transferred his passengers while *Tang*'s guns sank the capsized Kingfisher. Burns and Gill then took off to search for more aircrew from an airplane reported down near Kuop Reef on the eastern rim of Truk. When *Tang* arrived on the scene hours later the Kingfisher had almost a football team aboard.

Burns had been busy. He had rescued two full TBF crews and had all six of them clinging onto the airplane. Towing the men on a life raft had been tried but proved impractical owing to the amount of spray thrown back when the floatplane's engine was revved up and swamping the occupants. Now *Tang*, which had been delayed for some five hours due to an alert to pick up

yet another downed flyer, found a very waterlogged Kingfisher, listing under the weight of its human cargo.

When everyone was aboard, *Tang* had plucked a total of 22 airmen from the ocean in two days of Truk raids. And according to *Tang*'s illustrious skipper, Lieutenant Commander Richard H. O'Kane, the Kingfisher pilot was very sad at losing his aircraft:

"We sent Burns below so he couldn't see and we sank the plane with gunfire."

The loss of *North Carolina*'s two OS2Us at Truk showed that shipboard floatplane attrition rates could be high. For the record, the original three dash 2 models had arrived aboard in May 1941, a month after the ship was commissioned. These were BuAer Nos. 2288 (which arrived aboard on 10 May), 3073 (13 May) and 3074 (15 May).[2]

On 22 October 1944 the first SC-1 Seahawk was embarked on the *Guam* to begin the closing chapter of US floatplane operations. Battleship and cruiser skippers appreciated the modest amount of space that a

A "thumbs up" indicates that the pilot is highly satisfied with an early test flight in the SC-1 Seahawk. An entirely new concept in shipboard scout planes, the SC gave aviators fighter-like performance but its single seat all but precluded rescue work. (via Aeroplane Monthly)

"folded" Seahawk took up and pilots suddenly found they had an airplane with an impressive performance.

Combat Swansong

Although US shipboard floatplanes had been exposed to enemy fighter interception during Atlantic operations, this remained a relatively isolated occurrence considering the number of spotting flights carried out during the US Navy's "two-ocean war". In the Pacific, the instances of attack by Japanese fighters remained mercifully rare, as few aviators would have given much for their chances. But on 16 February 1945, three days before the troops went ashore on Iwo Jima, one of *Pensacola*'s OS2Us survived the aggressive attention of a Zeke 52 and turned a highly dangerous situation to fine advantage. The Kingfisher, piloted by Lieutenant (j.g.) Douglas W. Gandy, was flying at 1,500 feet directing pre-invasion gunfire on the northern end of Iwo. At 0213 a patrolling Zeke dived on the OS2U, fired a short burst and broke tightly away.

Gandy followed. He dived and turned, bringing his aircraft onto the Zeke's tail, about 500 feet astern. Snapping out long bursts from his single .30-caliber front gun, Gandy saw his fire strike the enemy fighter's cockpit, engine and right wing root. A thin stream of smoke appeared and Gandy went in for the *coup de grace*. Another turn, another long burst. The Zeke half-rolled to the right, burst into flames and crashed into the island. Scooting away at 1,000 feet, the OS2U drew heavy fire from Japanese ground troops, all of which fortunately missed.

Lt. (j.g.) Doug Gandy, is decorated by the Captain of *Pensacola* after his feat of airmanship in downing a Zeke. (Ray Snapp)

As the US Navy stormed across the Pacific to virtually isolate Japan, a number of actions and incidents broke the general routine of floatplane operations. A few highlighted their known vulnerability and led to a growing belief that their usefulness had all but passed. Some skippers would willingly have disposed of spotter planes there and then. Officialdom thought otherwise. They stayed.

Among the reasons why they did was demonstrated on 18 March 1945 when one of the *New Jersey*'s OS2Us flown by Lieutenant W. A. Ethridge, plucked a *Bunker Hill* pilot out of the water off Kyushu. In a heavy swell, the Kingfisher did well to complete the rescue successfully.

Adverse sea conditions affected all vessels and the more there were in a task group, the greater was the collision risk. Sailors on ships obliged to keep station with the mighty battleships of the *Iowa* Class were always wary – they would invariably come off worse if the hulls touched. But not always: all the fast battleships carried their two OS2Us on the fantail and during the spring of 1945 the destroyer *Welles* on mail call came too close to the *New Jersey* and wrecked a Kingfisher. It was stripped of all usable parts and dumped into the sea.

On 24 March spotter aircraft from *New Jersey*, *Wisconsin* and *Missouri* combined to orchestrate a spectacular main battery bombardment of Okinawa in support of the US landing. *Missouri*, by then re-equipped with the SC-1, sent her spotters over the island and lost an aircraft to AA fire. The replacement airplane did not last long when during transfer from the USS *Guam* the Seahawk's propeller fouled the crane. With the enemy on the run, little time could be spared for repairs and once again a battleship floatplane was given the "deep six". Destroyers sank the SC with gunfire.

New Jersey finished her war operations with a "live" practice shoot on Wake Island which was still occupied by the Japanese. A leisurely affair which included a lunch break, the battleship received some answering fire from the enemy guns but apart from one or two holes in one of her floatplanes, no harm was done.

Early in 1945 some US cruisers were undergoing refits and modernization in preparation for the last big operation of the war – the invasion of Japan. In general these changes focused on increasing AA defense against kamikazes, which meant weight saving in other areas. Consequently, one catapult was removed from all 10,000 ton heavy and light cruisers still in service and prewar vessels which had carried three spotter planes, henceforth carried two.

Only the flagship *Indianapolis* kept her three aircraft, SOCs having by that time been replaced by SC-1s, although she too had had one of her catapults removed. All floatplanes were lost when the cruiser was torpedoed by the Japanese submarine I-58 on 29 July 1945. Among the countless acts of bravery in the aftermath of that tragedy Airman 1st Class Anthony Maday

Pensacola took some fire during the Iwo Jima operation, Japanese shore batteries scoring a direct hit amidships. One of the cruiser's OS2Us poised on the starboard catapult was completely wrecked. (Ray Snapp)

was cited for his assistance to the wounded while awaiting rescue. He was recommended for the Bronze Star.

Another successful rescue of a downed pilot was accomplished on 9 August. While attacking Ominato airfield on northern Honshu as part of a strike from the carrier *Essex*, Lieutenant (j.g.) Vernon Coumbre's F4U Corsair was hit by flak. He managed to nurse the crippled fighter five miles out to sea and ditch. Apparently unseen by the enemy, Coumbre's life raft was determinedly drifting toward the shore. There was no way to stop it and when it beached, the pilot took to the tree line. Meanwhile, other aircraft from the *Essex* roared overhead, searching for their downed comrade. Coumbre was spotted and his position relayed to the fleet.

Aboard the *North Carolina,* Lieutenant Ralph Jacobs and Lieutenant (j.g.) Almon Oliver volunteered to get Coumbre. The OS2Us were launched around 2000, each airplane with an empty rear seat ready for the passenger, if they could locate him. Escorted by F4Us from the *Essex* the Kingfishers flew at 200 feet to avoid Japanese radar.

An hour and ten minutes later, Jacobs and Oliver were over Ominato. They saw Coumbre and one of the F4Us promptly dived to drop him a raft. The floatplane pilots watched, horrified, as the Corsair pilot misjudged his speed and spun into the ocean. No trace of him or his airplane were seen.

Jacobs landed to pick up Coumbre, who waded out against the breakers. Standing up to toss out a line, Jacobs was precariously balanced with one foot on the wing and the other in the cockpit. Then a wave struck the Kingfisher and tipped it violently. As he fell, Jacobs'

foot hit the throttle and the Kingfisher promptly careened off out to sea . . . without a pilot.

Japanese gunners had seen the floatplane and opened up with artillery. The Corsair pilots thought the rescue had happened until they saw the OS2U's empty cockpit. Circling in the second floatplane, Oliver was told to land and get Coumbre; another plane would return for Jacobs.

The second OS2U touched down - and both men clambered aboard to squeeze into the rear cockpit. Oliver gunned the engine and the floatplane lifted off. All hell broke loose below as the enemy gunners bracketed the runaway Kingfisher, which was finally sunk by the F4Us.

Thankfully back aboard the "Showboat", the intrepid pilots were told that Oliver's OS2U had just two minutes' fuel left in its tanks. Jacobs and Oliver received the DFC for their rescue feat but the best news of the day came around 2100 hours - Japan had indicated her willingness to surrender.

Although hostilities ceased on 15 August 1945 it was not until 2 September that the official surrender ceremony took place, aboard the *Missouri*. Perhaps fittingly, the best vantage point was taken by the battleship's senior aviator. This very thin individual was able to squeeze into the range finder of No 2 gun turret and use his camera to record the events going on directly below him – an experience he was well used to! [3]

Active units of the US fleet large enough to carry aircraft – where this was still deemed necessary – went over to the SC-1 for early postwar duty. Other ships which had been intended to carry aircraft, never received them but the ever-useful fantail cranes designed for lifting floatplanes remained in most cases.

Lieutenant (j.g.) A. Lee Perry, who also flew the N3N and OS2U, gained considerable experience with the SC-1, flying the latter from the 14,000-ton *Baltimore* Class cruiser *Bremerton* (CA-130) in the immediate postwar period. The ship was commissioned on 29 April 1945 and sailed on her shakedown cruise on 29 May, bound for the waters off Guantanamo Bay, Cuba, carrying two SC-1s. Lee Perry retains vivid recollections of his service in floatplanes, particularly the SC.

"Being a single seater, there was no dual instruction prior to flying the SC – just one week's ground school. My first take off, in a section of four aircraft, was a revelation. We turned into wind. My buddy and fellow pilot, Will W. Gildner, went first, in a blast of water and spray. I was next and figured if he could, I could . . .

"We had been warned about the excess power compared to the OS2U, so I advanced the throttle cautiously. At about two-thirds power the plane jumped off the water after traveling about 200 feet! It continued to climb at a 45 degree angle before I had the presence of mind to throttle back and level off. Having been airborne at about 70 kts, the SC quickly accelerated to 100 kts in the climb. I was slightly shocked - it was a dramatic change from the OS.

Young Ensign Seahawk aviators W. Gildner and Lee Perry (right) with an SC at Guantanimo Bay, Cuba. (A. Lee Perry)

"It also was more maneuverable, with much quicker response, better control and visibility; landing presented no real problem, at least in daylight. But the SC was not of course perfect; its design precluded a full stall landing and you had to keep some power on to keep the nose up until water contact, otherwise the nose would 'fall through' and probably dive into a wave and flip over. Several accidents occurred and it was later banned from night flying, mainly for this drawback which was due, I believe, to the center of gravity being forward of the cockpit.

"Among the SC's other bad habits was a tendency for the auto pilot (after it had been switched off) to start 'grabbing' the controls. We solved that by permanently disconnecting the auto-pilot but could do little about the turbo supercharger throwing blades when it was engaged above 10,000 ft - very hazardous to health!

"Also, the radar we carried - in a pod under the right wing - was less than satisfactory. It required looking into a cockpit hood about a foot below normal eye level and it took time to adjust to the dark while you were still flying the plane. The PPI scope was difficult to tune properly to get the right fix and after a time we generally gave up on it. The radar worked fine on the ship, in the shop, on land and for an experienced radar operator with nothing else to do – but for us, no way. The plastic radar housing was very subject to salt air and water corrosion damage due to heavy sea landings, necessitating constant service and overhaul. And yet we felt the SC to be vastly superior to the OS2U and a joy to fly on its designated spotting, reconnaissance and ASR tasks.

"Launch procedure for the *Bremerton*'s SCs followed a routine well practiced in the Navy by the time she joined the fleet. We pilots would come to the fantail after briefing. Two planes would be warming up on the catapults with the crew making last minute checks.

"We would have a brief chat with the launch officer and plane captain and when assured that everything was OK we'd climb the ladder to the cockpit. While the plane captain helped with the straps, you started on the cockpit check list. This included comparing the SC's magnetic compass reading with the ship's course and noting the deviation and locking the plot board under the dashboard, out of the way.

"With everything running smoothly you throttled back to idle (800-1,000 rpm) and gave a thumb up launch signal. The plane captain communicated that the plane was ready for launch to the bridge and repeated this, followed by the "one finger" run up signal. The pilot slowly advanced the throttle to maximum revs, held it there and made sure that manifold pressure, cylinder head temperature, oil pressure and so on were as they should be by getting a green

Bremerton launches one of her SCs during a postwar cruise. (A. Lee Perry)

Lee Perry flying "Devil's Kitten", the *Bremerton's* No. 3 SC-1 with a spiral decoration on its propeller boss, off the Culebra Islands. (A. Lee Perry)

Although they were hardly elaborate, floatplane identification markings were quite varied, particularly in the immediate postwar period. These ramp-bound SC-1s of SOSU-3 at Alameda NAS have large size "W" prefix fuselage and underwing codes, "W9", "W20", "W43" and "W28" being visible. The latter Seahawk, unlike the others, has the overall sea blue color scheme. (A. Lee Perry)

Fantail view of the USS *Boston*'s three SC-1s in May 1945. Note how compact the aircraft was in fully folded condition. (National Archives 80-G-378960)

shading on the relevant dials. The throttle was brought back to idle and the pilot made the thumb up signal again.

"The catapult was trained out about 30 to 40 degrees from the ship's centerline and a turn into "relative wind" (not true wind) was made. What the pilot looked for was the wind direction indicator at the front end of the catapult lining up directly parallel with the catapult. When the ship was steady on the relative wind course, the launch officer gave the two finger "run up", ready to launch signal.

"Full power. Left hand on the throttle lock to prevent it springing back under the launch shock. Head back against the padded seat headrest. Try to think above the deafening roar of the engine and the incredible vibration and wait for the first convenient roll the ship makes down or toward you. As the ship starts to recover and roll back in the opposite direction the catapult officer fires the aircraft off. This careful timing ensured that the plane went off with the catapult level.

"The pressure shock imposed 7-8G on the SC pilot, a thing that a man got used to surprisingly quickly. At the average wind speed at sea of 10-15kts, the ship increased speed: 20-25-30 kts - to give the floatplane pilot a minimum airspeed of 80 kts, about 10 kts above stalling speed for the SC.

"Once safe flying speed had been attained the SC pilot came back on the throttle to 2,800 rpm and climbed at round 100 kts at 500 feet. Single planes circled the ship unless there was a wingman along for a final check and the mission was underway."

A successful launch clearly disappointed the ship's company most of whom would foregather to watch:

"When flight operations were announced over the *Bremerton*'s PA system, sailors we hadn't seen for weeks came topside out of the bowels of the ship to see the 'show'. The crowd on the aft quarter of the main deck was so great that a rope barrier was erected across the fantail to restrain the spectators from getting too close to the catapult. It was like we cheated them of some spectacular entertainment; such can be the boredom of shipboard life . . ."

Recovery

Long experience in operating spotter planes from ships had developed four standard procedures for floatplane recovery which were code named Able, Baker, Charlie and Dog. The first two were reserved for recovery with the ship at anchor or alongside a dock; Charlie was the most common underway recovery using the sled under normal sea conditions and Dog a variation adopted in calm "no wind" conditions, also with the ship underway. Charlie recovery of her SCs by the *Bremerton* was as follows:

On returning to the ship, the SC circled left at 300 feet, counter-clockwise. On the downwind leg, the pilot watched the signal bridge for the recovery flag "at the dip", i.e. half mast. As the plane flew abeam the ship the flag went "two block", to the top of the mast, the "execute" signal to land.

The ship was ready to recover at that point and began a turn into the wind. The airplane cut power, dropped flaps and made a sharp left turn calculated to reach the water abreast of the ship's starboard stern quarter. The ship turned to the right through the prevailing wind and sea to create a slick, a crescent-shaped calm area of water on the inside of the turn. In effect the ship became a moving breakwater making about 10-15 kts.

The floatplane touched down on this calm water and taxied alongside the stern quarter while the ship streamed a sled from the starboard catapult which was trained outboard. The floatplane taxied onto the sled, a 9x12 foot mat with a cork bow to keep it buoyant. The pilot watched the catapult officer's signal flags - necessary because the aircraft's nose hid the sled from view. When the airplane was securely on the sled the cat officer indicated "Roger" with both his arms horizontal.

Reducing power until he felt the hook on the main float snag/engage the cargo net on the sled, the pilot watched for the "cut power" signal (hand sliced across the cat officer's throat). With the engine off, the SC pilot pulled a lanyard in the cockpit to open the door of a small fuselage compartment in front of the wind-

shield, reached over the windshield and released a coiled steel cable hoist. Meanwhile, the ship's crane crew had swung their hook out over the SC. The pilot grabbed the rope attached to the hook and guided it down to engage the plane lift cable. A thumbs up indicated that the crane crew should lift the airplane and place it on the catapult.

Surprisingly, the most difficult airplane recovery was the Dog. Lee Perry's first was during the *Bremerton's* shakedown cruise. Off Guantanamo Bay, she became the flagship of Admiral Jonas Ingram, C-in-C Atlantic Fleet, for his South American tour of inspection. This included evaluating the *Bremerton's* combat efficiency.

After flying a main battery spotting sortie, Lee Perry who then had about 50 hours SC time but had not made a shipboard recovery in that type of airplane, was

Interesting view from the mainmast of the old battleship *New York* (BB-34) in February 1946 shows three SC-1s, one of which has yet to be assembled. The aircraft in the foreground is mounted on the turret catapult. (USN)

This SC-1 launch from the *Might Mo* on 27 February 1948 was almost certainly, "according to the Navy photo caption, the last observation plane sortie from a US battleship. Ensign F. H. Gilkie is the pilot. (National Archives)

horrified to see the sea state. There was no wind and the sea was like a sheet of glass. Zero wind conditions at sea are rare and dangerous for floatplane recovery, especially for an inexperienced pilot. Used to allowing for wind, the pilot can easily forget to compensate for a total lack of it. Misjudging height and losing depth perception is a very real danger in such a situation.

Undaunted, the SC came in to receive a Charlie recovery signal, Lee Perry assuming that this was to demonstrate the standard technique to the admiral . . .

"As I approached the landing slick, the plane would not slow down, stall or land as I reduced power. It floated on a cushion of rising hot air and flew straight at the ship's side. At the last possible second, I kicked the rudder and shoved the stick hard left. The SC slid under the counter (stern) and landed on the other (left) side of the ship. I think the right wing tip missed the stern by about ten feet – very embarrassing!

"After the recovery the senior aviator summarized my unacceptable performance and said the captain was very upset. Apparently he and the admiral had been observing the recovery from the flying bridge. When the captain saw me disappear under the stern of the ship, he bolted through a passageway linking the starboard and port wings of the bridge, tripped over two talkers sitting on the deck, lost his hat and crawled to a nearby guntub. He peered over the armour shield to see if I missed the ship. The admiral was far from impressed.

"This incident almost repeated itself later in mid-Pacific. There was no wind, sea like a silvered mirror with the sun setting. I fell in behind Will Gildner, circling the ship at 300 feet. The Dog signal went up and he made to land parallel with the ship close abeam the starboard side. I watched . . . he over-

shot the amidships landing spot and his airplane dropped like a rock off the bow quarter in a tremendous circular pattern splash. He taxied over to the sled and was recovered.

"I got the D signal and went down. As I approached amidships I had to keep coming back on the power and stick, raise the nose and wait for water contact. But it was the same as Guantanamo. The SC just floated over the glassy sea. More power, more stick. The stick hit the front edge of my seat, which had never happened before. At that instant the airplane dropped 5-10 feet like a rock.

"I tried to break the fall with max power, to hold the nose up but the engine backfired and the prop windmilled. Out of the corner of my eye I saw the gas mixture control in 'auto-lean' instead of 'auto-rich', which it should have been prior to landing.

"I hit the water 'flat' with a helluva splash. Luckily the float's nose was up and did not dive in. I taxied over to the ship and the wrath of the senior aviator. There was no damage to the plane - but my pride was wounded. Some time later, I was acting as on-board aviation talker when the word came down from the bridge to secure for the day and recover airplanes. I relayed the order to the quartermaster who manned the ship's PA system. Shortly came the message: 'Now hear this - all aviation personnel lay aft to the fantail and prepare to recover two aircraft 'Doggie fashion'. The hoots, howls and screams of laughter could be heard throughout the ship."

So, with peace, the mighty US fleet was gradually reduced under stringent economies. Within the next three decades most of the wartime cruisers were stricken or sold and sadly, none survived intact as a permanent memorial. A similar fate awaited most of the battleships, only the *Iowa* Class surviving to see further combat. When Ensign F. H. Gilkie was launched in an SC-1 from the fantail of the *Missouri* on 27 February 1948, the era of the shipboard floatplane in the US Navy finally came to a close. [4]

Happily, the wartime floatplanes did not all go the way of the majority of their parent ships. Among the ever-growing number of preserved aircraft are OS2Us, two of which are mounted aboard ships. The USS *North Carolina* at Wilmington has her Kingfisher positioned forward while the other graces the fantail of the *Alabama* at Mobile.

Notes:
1. See note, chapter 2.
2. Sitting Duck; *North Carolina's* Kingfisher: USS *North Carolina* Battleship Commission.
3. Muir, Malcolm: The *Iowa* Class Battleships; Blandford Press 1987.
4. Ibid.

In 1970 Vought Aeronautics personnel expertly reconstructed an OS2U-2 recovered from Calvert Island, British Colombia in 1963. On completion of an 11-month rebuild the Kingfisher, which had crashed during the Aleutian campaign on 20 August 1942, was duly photographed with a later and slightly faster company product, an A-7E. The Kingfisher now rests aboard the *North Carolina* at the Patriots Point Naval Museum, Charleston, SC. (Vought PR 32118)

APPENDIX 1

AIRCRAFT SPECIFICATIONS
CURTISS SOC SEAGULL
TYPE: Biplane scout/observation floatplane
ACCOMMODATION: Pilot and observer
POWERPLANT: One 600 HP Pratt & Whitney R-1340-18 radial
DIMENSIONS: Span 36 ft; length 31 ft 5 in; height 14 ft 9 in; wing area 342 sq ft
WEIGHTS: Empty 3,788 lb; gross 5,437 lb
PERFORMANCE: Maximum speed 165 mph; cruise 133 mph; service ceiling 14,900 ft; range 675 st miles
ARMAMENT: One fixed forward-firing 0.30-in machine gun in wing and one 0.30-in MG on flexible mount in rear cockpit; two x 325 lb bombs or depth charges on underwing racks
SERIAL NUMBERS: X03C-1: 9413; SOC-1: 9856-9990; SOC-3: 1064-1146; SOC-4: V171-173 (48243-48245); SON-1: 1147-1190

GRUMMAN J2F DUCK
TYPE: Biplane utility amphibian
ACCOMMODATION: Pilot, observer and (optional) radio operator
POWERPLANT: One 950 hp Wright R-1820-50 radial
DIMENSIONS: Span 39 ft; length 34 ft; height 15 ft 1 in; wing area 409 sq ft
WEIGHTS: Empty 4,300 lb; gross 6,711 lb
PERFORMANCE: Max speed 188 mph; cruise 150 mph; service ceiling 27,000 ft; range 780 st miles
ARMAMENT: Optional 0.30-in MG on flexible mount in rear cockpit and up to 325 lb of ordnance on wing racks
SERIAL NUMBERS: XJF-1: 9218; JF-1: 9434-9455/9523-9527; JF-2: V161-V175*; JF-3: 9835-9839; J2F-1: 0162-0190; J2F-2: 0780-0794/ 1195-1197/ 1207-1209; J2F-2A: 1198-1206; J2F-3: 1568-1587; J2F-4: 1639-1670; J2F-5: 00659-00802; Colombia J2F-6: 32637-32786/ 33535-33614/ 36935-37034
* Renumbered V135 to V148 in 1936; original V175 to USMC as 0266.

VOUGHT OS2U KINGFISHER
TYPE: Monoplane observation-scout floatplane
ACCOMMODATION: Pilot and observer/gunner
POWERPLANT: One 459 hp Pratt & Whitney R-985-AN-2 or -8 Wasp Junior radial
DIMENSIONS: Span 35 ft 10 in; length 33 ft 10 in; height 15 ft 1 in; wing area 262 sq ft
WEIGHTS: Empty 4,123 lb; gross 6,000 lb
PERFORMANCE: Max speed 164 mph; cruise 119 mph; ceiling 13,000 ft; range 805 st miles
ARMAMENT: One fixed 0.30-in MG firing through starboard side of engine and one flexible 0.30-in MG in rear cockpit
SERIAL NUMBERS: XOSU-1: 0951; OS2U-1: 1681-1734; OS2U-2: 2189-2288/ 3073-3130; OS2U-3: 5284-5989/ 09393-09692; NAF OS2N-1: 01216-01515

CURTISS SC-1 SEAHAWK
TYPE: Monoplane scout/ ASW floatplane
ACCOMMODATION: Pilot
POWERPLANT: One 1,350 hp Wright R-1820-62 radial
DIMENSIONS: Span 41 ft; length 36 ft 4 in; height 16 ft; wing area 280 sq ft
WEIGHTS: Empty 6,320 lb; gross 9,000 lb
PERFORMANCE: Max speed 313 mph; cruise 125 mph; service ceiling 27,300 ft; range 625 st miles
ARMAMENT: Two fixed 0.50-in machine guns in wings; up to 325 lb cf ordnance on wing stations; optional bomb cell in central float
SERIAL NUMBERS: XSC-1: 35298-35300; SC-1: 35301-35797/ 93302-93367; SC-2: 119529-119538

APPENDIX 1 (cont.)

CURTISS SO3C SEAGULL/SEAMEW
TYPE: Monoplane scout/observation floatplane
ACCOMMODATION: Pilot and observer
POWERPLANT: One 600 hp Ranger V -770-8 in-line
DIMENSIONS: Span 38 ft; length 35 ft 8 in; height 14 ft 2 in; wing area 293 sq ft
WEIGHTS: Empty 4,800 lb; gross 7,000 lb
PERFORMANCE: Max speed 172 mph; cruise 125 mph; service ceiling 15,800 ft; range 1,150 st miles
ARMAMENT: One fixed 0.30 in MG forward plus one 0.50-in flexible MG in rear cockpit; up to 325 lb ordnance under each wing and up to 325 lb under fuselage
SERIAL NUMBERS: XO3C-1: 1385; SO3C-1: 4730-4783/4793-4879; SO3C-2: 4880-5029/ 04149-04198; SO3C-2C: 4784-4792/ 22007-22256; SO3C-3: 04199-04348

APPENDIX 2
US NAVY INSHORE PATROL SQUADRONS

OLD NO	BASE	NEW DESIG-NATION*	WARTIME BASE(S) WHERE APPLICABLE
VS-1D1	Squantum, MS	VS-31	
VS-1D3	New York, NY	VS-34	
VS-1D4	Cape May, NJ	VS-35	
VS-1D5	Norfolk, VA	VS-37	
VS-1D7	Banana River	VS-39	
VS-1D10	San Juan, PR	VS-63	
VS-1D11	San Pedro, CA	VS-46	
VS-1D12	Alameda, CA	VS-47	
VS-1D13	Terminal Is, CA	VS-49	
VS-1D15	Coco Solo, Panama	VS-59	
VS-2D1	Quonset Pt., RI	VS-32	
VS-2D5	Norfolk, VA	VS-38	
VS-2D7	Key West, FL	VS-40	
VS-2D10	Guantanamo, Cuba	VS-43	
VS-2D13	Seattle, WA	VS-50	Kodiak, AL
VS-2D14	San Diego, CA	VS-51	
VS-2D14	Quonset Pt., RI	VS-52	Bora Bora
VS-2D14	Alameda, CA	VS-54	
VS-2D15	Coco Solo, Panama	VS-60	
VS-3D1	Quonset Pt., RI	VS-33	
VS-3D7	Key West, FL	VS-62	
VS-3D10	San Juan, PR	VS-44	
VS-3D14	Pearl Harbor, HI	VS-53	
VS-4D10	Port of Spain, Trinidad	VS-45	
VS-5D4	Cape May, NJ	VS-36	
VS-5D14	Alameda, CA	VS-55	Espirito Santo, New Hebrides
VS-6D14	Alameda, CA	VS-56	Adak, AK
VS-7D14	Alameda, CA	VS-57	
VS-8D14	Alameda, CA	VS-58	
		VS-64	Florida Isl, Guadalcanal
		VS-68	Ugi Island.
		VS-65	
		VS-66	

*Effective 1 March 1943

APPENDIX 2 (Cont)

Note: The letter "D" in the original designations denoted the Naval District to which the unit(s) were assigned, i.e. VS-1D4 was Scouting Squadron One, Fourth Naval District.

U.S. Marine Corps

J2F-5s attached to combat units included:
VMF-111; VMF-123; VMF-212; VMF-224; VMF-252; VMO-155; VMO-251; VMJ-253; HQ Sqdn 2nd MAW; VMSB-151; VMS-3
OS2N-1: VMS-3 (St. Thomas, Virgin Islands)
NB: J2Fs were invariably in inventories of headquarters squadrons in each of the active Marine Air Wings.

APPENDIX 3
FLOATPLANES WITH THE FLEET, WW II

SHIP	AIRCRAFT	CATAPULT LOCATION	COMMISSIONING DATE	REMARKS
BATTLESHIPS				
Arkansas (BB-33)	3 x OS2U	1-AS	17 Sept 12	Atl/Pac
TEXAS CLASS				
New York (BB-34)	3 x OS2U/SOC/SC-1	1-AS	15 Apr 13	Atl/Pac
Texas (BB-35)	3 x OS2U/SOC/OS2U	1-AS	12 Mar 14	Atl/Pac
OKLAHOMA CLASS				
Nevada (BB-36)	3 x OS2U	2 (1-F/1-AS)*	11 Mar 16	Pac/Atl
Oklahoma (BB-37)	3 x SOC/OS2U	2 (1-AS/1-F)	02 May 16	Pac: WL 7 Dec 41
PENNSYLVANIA CLASS				
Pennsylvania (BB-38)	3 x OS2U/SC-1	1-F	12 Jun 16	Pac
Arizona (BB-39)	3 x OS2U	2 (1-AS/1-F)	17 Oct 16	Pac: WL 7 Dec 41
NEW MEXICO CLASS				
New Mexico (BB-40)	3 x OS2U	1-F	10 May 18	Pac
Mississippi (BB-41)	4 x OS2U	2 (1-F/1-AS)*	18 Dec 17	Pac
Idaho (BB-42)	3 x OS2U	1-F	24 Mar 19	Pac
* Catapult over No 3 turret removed during wartime refit				
CALIFORNIA CLASS				
Tennessee (BB-43)	3 x OS2U	1 AS/1-F*	03 Jun 20	Pac
California (BB-44	4 x OS2U/SC-1	2-AS	10 Aug 21	Pac
*One catapult removed during wartime refit				
MARYLAND CLASS				
Colorado (BB-45)	3 x OS2U	2-F*	30 Aug 23	Pac
Maryland (BB-46)	3 x OS2U	1-AS	21 Jul 21	Pac
West Virginia (BB-48)	3 x OS2U	1-F	01 Dec 23	Pac
* Catapult over No 3 turret removed during wartime refit				
NORTH CAROLINA CLASS				
North Carolina (BB-55)	3 x OS2U/SO3C/OS2U	2-F*	09 Apr 41	Atl/Pac
Washington (BB-56)	3 x OS2U	2-F	15 May 41	At./Pac
* One catapult removed, 1945				
SOUTH DAKOTA CLASS				
South Dakota (BB-57)	3 x OS2U	2-F	20 Mar 42	Pac/Atl
Indiana (BB-58)	3 x OS2U	2-F	30 Apr 42	Pac
Massachusetts (BB-59)	3 x OS2U/SOC	2-F	12 May 42	Atl/Pac
Alabama (BB-60)	3 x OS2U/SC-1	2-F	16 Aug 42	Atl/Pac
IOWA CLASS				
Iowa (BB-61)	3 x OS2U/SC-1	2-F	22 Feb 43	Pac
New Jersey (BB-62)	3 x OS2U/SC-1	2-F	02 May 43	Pac
Missouri (BB-63)	3 x OS2U/SC-1	2-F	11 Jun 44	Pac
Wisconsin (BB-64)	3 x OS2U/SC-1	2-F	16 Apr 44	Pac
BATTLE CRUISERS				
ALASKA CLASS				
Alaska (CB-1)	4 x SO3C/OS2U*/SC-1	2-mid	17 Jun 44	Pac
Guam (CB-2)	4 x OS2U*/SC-1	2-mid	17 Sep 44	Pac
* One catapult removed during wartime refit				
HEAVY CRUISERS				
PENSACOLA CLASS				
Pensacola (CA-24)	4 x SOC/OS2U/SC-1	2-mid	06 Feb 30	Pac
Salt Lake City (CA-25)	4 x SOC/OS2U	2-mid	11 Dec 29	Pac
NORTHAMPTON CLASS				
Northampton (CA-26)	4 x SOC	2-mid	17 May 30	Pac: WL 1 Dec 42
Chester (CA-27)	3 x OS2U	2-mid	24 Jun 30	Pac
Louisville (CA-28)	3 x SOC	2-mid	15 Jan 31	Pac
Chicago (CA-29)	3 x SOC	2-mid	09 Mar 31	Pac: WL 30 Jan 43
Houston (CA-30)	4 x SOC	2-mid	17 Jun 30	Pac: WL 1 Mar 42
Augusta (CA-31)	4 x SOC	2-mid	30 Jan 31	Atl

APPENDIX 3 (Cont.)

		CATAPULT LOCATION	COMMISSIONING DATE	REMARKS
INDIANAPOLIS CLASS				
Portland (CA-33)	3 x SOC	2-mid	23 Feb 33	Pac
Indianapolis (CA-35)	3 x SOC/SC-1	2-mid*	15 Nov 32	Pac: WL 29 Jul 45
* One catapult removed during wartime refit				
ASTORIA CLASS				
New Orleans (CA-32)	4 x SOC	2-AS	15 Feb 34	Pac
Astoria (CA-34)	4 x SOC/OS2U	2-AS	28 Apr 34	Pac: WL 9 Aug 42
Minneapolis (CA-36)	4 x SOC	2-AS	19 May 34	Pac
Tuscaloosa (CA-37)	4 x SOC/ 3 x SC-1	2-AS	17 Aug 34	Atl/Pac
San Francisco (CA-38)	4 x SOC	2-AS	10 Feb 34	Pac/Atl
Quincy (CA-39)	4 x SOC	2-AS	09 Jun 36	Atl/Pac: WL 9 Aug 42
Vincennes (CA-44)	4 x SOC/OS2U	2-F	24 Feb 37	Atl/Pac: WL 9 Aug 42
WICHITA CLASS				
Wichita (CA-45)	4 x SOC	2-F	16 Feb 39	Atl/Pac
BALTIMORE CLASS				
Baltimore (CA-68)	4 x OS2U	2-F	15 Apr 43	Atl/Pac
Boston (CA-69)	4 x OS2U/SO3C/SC-1	2-F	30 Jan 43	Pac
Canberra (CA-70)	4 x OS2U	2-F	14 Oct 43	Pac
Quincy (CA-71)	4 x OS2U	2-F	15 Dec 43	Pac
Pittsburgh (CA-72)	4 x SOC*/OS2U	2-F	10 Oct 44	Pac
St. Paul (CA-73)	4 x SC-1	2-F	17 Feb 45	Pac
Columbus (CA-74)	4 x SC-1	2-F	08 Jun 45	Pac
Helena (CA-75)	4 x SC-1	2-F	04 Sep 45	PW
Oregon City (CA-122)	4 x SC-1	2-F	16 Feb 46	PW
Albany (CA-123)	4 x SC-1	2-F	15 Jun 46	PW
Rochester (CA-124)*	none	–	20 Dec 46	PW
Northampton (CA-125)*	none	–	07 Mar 53	PW
Bremerton (CA-130)	2 x SC -1	2-F	29 Apr 45	PW
Fall River (CA-131)	2 x SC-1	2-F	01 Jul 45	PW
Macon (CA-132)	2 x SC-1	2-F	26 Aug 45	PW
Los Angeles (CA-135)	2 x SC-1	2-F	22 July 45	PW
Chicago (CA-136)	4 x SC-1	2-F	10 Jan 45	Pac
DES MOINES CLASS				
Des Moines (CA-134)*	none	–	16 Nov 48	PW
Salem (CA-139)*	none	–	14 May 49	PW
Newport News (CA-148)*	none	–	29 Jan 49	PW

*Believed commissioned without ever having aircraft embarked; catapults were removed early in each ships' service, only cranes being retained.

LIGHT CRUISERS

		CATAPULT LOCATION	COMMISSIONING DATE	REMARKS
OMAHA CLASS				
Omaha (CL-4)	2 x SOC/OS2U*	2-AS	24 Feb 23	Atl
Milwaukee (CL-5)	2 x SOC/OS2U*	2-AS	20 Jun 23	Atl
Cincinnati (CL-6)	2 x SOC/OS2U*	2-AS	01 Jan 24	Atl
Raleigh (CL-7)	2 x SOC/OS2U*	2-AS	06 Feb 24	Pac
Detroit (CL-8)	2 x SOC/OS2U	2-AS	31 Jul 23	Pac
Richmond (CL-9)	2 x OS2U	2-AS	02 Jul 23	Pac
Concord (CL-10)	2 x SOC/J2F**	2-AS	03 Nov 23	Pac
Trenton (CL-11)	2 x SOC/OS2U	2-AS	19 Apr 24	Pac
Marblehead (CL-12)	2 x SOC/OS2U	2-AS	08 Sep 24	Pac/Atl
Memphis (CL-13)	2 x SOC/OS2U	2-AS	04 Feb 25	Atl

** J2F Duck used for Nov 1943 base examination cruise

		CATAPULT LOCATION	COMMISSIONING DATE	REMARKS
BROOKLYN CLASS				
Brooklyn (CL-40)	4 x SOC	2-F	30 Dep 37	Atl
Philadelphia (CL-41)	4 x SOC/OS2U	2-F	23 Sep 37	Atl/Pac
Savannah (CL-42)	4 x SOC/SC-1	2-F	10 Mar 38	Atl/Pac
Nashville (CL-43)	4 x SOC	2-F	06 Jun 38	Pac
Phoenix (CL-46)	4 x SOC	2-F	03 Oct 38	Atl/Pac
Boise (CL-47)	4 x SOC	2-F	12 Aug 38	Atl/Pac/Atl
Honolulu (CL-48)	4 x SOC	2-F	15 Jun 38	Atl/Pac
St. Louis (CL-49)	4 x SOC/OS2U	2-F	19 May 39	Pac
Helena (CL-50)	4 x SOC	2-F	18 Sep 39	Pac: WL 6 Jul 43
CLEVELAND - FARGO CLASS				
Cleveland (CL-55)	4 x SOC/SO3C/OS2U	2F/1-F	15 Jun 42	Atl/Pac
Columbia (CL-56)	4 x SOC/OS2U	2-F	29 Jul 42	Pac
Montpelier (CL-57)	4 x SOC/SO3C/ 2 x OS2U	2-F	09-Sep 42	Pac
Denver (CL-58)	4 x SOC/SO3C/SOC*	2-F	15 Oct 42	Pac
Santa Fe (CL-60)	4 x OS2U	2-AS	24 Nov 42	Pac
Birmingham (CL-62)	4 x OS2U	2-F	29 Jan 43	Atl/Pac

APPENDIX 3 (Cont.)

SHIP	AIRCRAFT	CATAPULT LOCATION	COMMISSIONING DATE	REMARKS
Mobile (CL-63)	4 x OS2U	2-F	24 Mar 43	Pac
Vincennes (CL-64)	4 x OS2U/SC-1	2-F	21 Jan 44	Pac
Pasadena (CL-65)	4 x OS2U/SC-1	2-F	08 Jun 44	Pac
Springfield (CL-66)	4 x OS2U	2-F	09 Sep 44	Pac
Topeka (CL-67)	4 x OS2U*/SC-1	2-F	23 Dec 44	Pac
Biloxi (CL-80)	4 x OS2U*	2-F	31 Aug 43	Pac
Houston (CL-81)	4 x OS2U	2-F	20 Dec 43	Pac
Providence (CL-82)	4 x SC-1	2-F	15 May 45	PW
Manchester (CL-83)	4 x SC-1	2-F	29 Oct 46	PW
Vicksburg (CL-86)	4 x OS2U	2-F	01 Jun 44	Pac
Duluth (CL-87)	4 x OS2U/SC-1	2-F	18 Sep 44	Pac
Miami (CL-89)	4 x OS2U/SC-1	2-F	28 Dec 43	Pac
Astoria (CL-90)	4 x OS2U/SC-1	2-F	17 May 44	Pac
Oklahoma City (CL-91)	4 x SO3C/OS2U*	2-F	17 May 44	Pac
Little Rock (CL-92)	4 x SC-1	2-F	22 Dec 44	PW
Amsterdam (CL-101)	4 x SC-1	2-F	08 Jan 45	Pac
Portsmouth (CL-102)	4 x SC-1	2-F	25 Jan 45	PW
Wilkes-Barre (CL-103)	4 x OS2U/SC-1*	2-F	01 Jul 44	Pac
Atlanta (CL-104)	4 x SC-1	2-F	03 Dec 44	Pac
Dayton (CL-105)	4 x SC-1	2-F	07 Jan 45	Pac
Fargo (CL-106)	4 x SC-1	2-F	09 Dec 45	PW
Huntingdon (CL-107)	4 x SC-1	2-F	23 Feb 46	PW

NB: In most if not all cases one catapult was removed from ships of this class for early post-war service; both catapults were ultimately removed.

WORCESTER CLASS

Worcester (CL-144)	none	2-F	26 Jun 48	PW
Roanoke (CL-145)	none	2-F	04 Apr 49	PW

Key F– fantail; mid – midships &/or abaft stack(s); AS – aft of stacks and on No 3 gun turret; WL – war loss; PW – mainly or entirely post-war service; Atl – Atlantic service; Pac – Pacific service.

The following ATLANTA/OAKLAND Class cruisers did not carry aircraft but are listed here for continuity purposes; *Atlanta* (CL-51) (WL 13 Nov 42); *Juneau* (CL-52) (WL 13 Nov 42); *San Diego* (CL-53); *San Juan* (CL-54); *Oakland* (CL-95); *Reno* (CL-96); *Flint* (CL-97); *Tucson* (CL-98); *Juneau* (CL-119); *Spokane* (CL-120); *Fresno* (CL-121).

Note 1. List includes ships commissioned many years prior to WW II and which carried early floatplane types not relevant here.
Note 2. Starboard catapult removed from all ships above 10,000 tons in 1945.
Note 3. Wherever possible, aircraft types quoted have been confirmed by photographic evidence.
Note 4. "No 3" turret refers to that positioned immediately aft of the main superstructure (reading from bow to stern).

* Indicates unconfirmed. Updates welcomed.

Even in calm weather, floatplanes had to be secured against violent pitching of the ship which could throw them off the catapult. Twin struts were used in securing the OS2U to the cradle prior to launching. (National Archives 80-G-378893)

A pre-war Kingfisher at Pensacola. (TZ Avn Photo via Jeff Ethell)

An OS2U-3 possibly at San Diego in 1942. (USN via Jeff Ethell)

Alaskan mountains form the backdrop for this 1943 Aleutian Kingfisher. (USN via Jeff Ethell)

OS2Us on the quarterdeck of *Missouri* during her 1944 shakedown cruise. (USN via Jeff Ethell)

Maintenance aboard BB *South Dakota* in 1944. The "kill" flag on the side of the OS2U represents an enemy horse bombed on Nauru Island. (USN via Jeff Ethell)

The crew of a Kingfisher (unit unknown) prepares to be brought aboard their ship somewhere in the Pacific, 1945. (USN via Jeff Ethell)

A Curtiss SOC-3 from the Atlantic Fleet in November 1942 carries Operation TORCH markings. The distinctive yellow roundel was used to help identify Allied aircraft involved in the joint British/American operation. The yellow ring may be judged a failure in as much as U.S. Navy aircraft downed an RAF photo-recon Spitfire and an RAF Hudson on anti-sub patrol.

The Navy's premier catapult float plane in World War II was the Vought Kingfisher. The OS2U-3 was used to observe its parent ships' "fall of shot", for over the horizon patrol, and anti-submarine patrol. But she became beloved among Naval aviators for her rescue services.

DEFINITIVE MILITARY/AVIATION HISTORIES
By
PHALANX PUBLISHING CO., LTD.

THE PINEAPPLE AIR FORCE: Pearl Harbor to Tokyo
by John Lambert $34.95

REPUBLIC P-47 THUNDERBOLT, The Final Chapter: Latin American Air Forces Service
by Dan Hagedorn $10.95

EAGLES OF DUXFORD: The 78th Fighter Group in World War II
by Garry Fry $22.95

KEARBY'S THUNDERBOLTS: The 348th Fighter Group in World War II
by John Stanaway $24.95

WILDCATS OVER CASABLANCA
by John Lambert $11.95

B-25 MITCHELL, The Magnificent Medium
by Norman L. Avery $29.95

SORTIE:
A bibliography of U.S. Air Force, Navy and Marine combat aviation unit histories from World War II.
Compiled by John W. Lambert $10.95

PACIFIC AIR COMBAT - Voices From The Past By Henry Sakaida $14.95

MESSERSCHMITT ROULETTE:
The Desert War from a Hurricane Recce Pilot of No 451 Squadron RAAF
Wing Commander Geoffrey Morley-Mower, RAF, (ret.), DFC $24 95

MARINE MITCHELLS
U.S. Marine Corps operations with PBJ aircraft in the Pacific, by Jerry Scutts. $12.95

THE 357TH OVER EUROPE
The 357th Fighter Group in Europe by Merle Olmsted $27.95

THE MARIANAS TURKEY SHOOT
 Carrier Battle in the Phillipine Sea by Barrett Tillman $12.95

SUN DOWNERS VF-11 in World War II by Barrett Tillman $12.95

"AN ESCORT OF P-38s": The First Fighter Group in World War II
The MTO war of this legendary P-38 unit by one of its pilots, John D. Mullins

FORTHCOMING TITLES

THE DESTRUCTION OF MARINE AIR GROUP 22
The sacrifice of Marine airmen on Midway Island, June 4-6, 1942, by Robert J. Cressman $12.95

PRIVATEERS The PB4Y-2 in World War II, by Nick Veronico

FROM HELLCATS TO TOMCATS: A Tale of Three Hookers
by Barrett Tillman with Zeke Cormier, Wally Schirra, and Phil Wood

BATMEN, The History of Night Air Group 90 in World War II by John MacLashing $12.95

The Gull Wing PZL: Volume 1, P-1 Through P-7 by Warren Eberspacher $12.95

The Fokker D.21: Volume 2, in Finnish Service by Warren Eberspacher $12.95